Pearson "Guide To"
Series in Business Communication

Guide to
Presentations

Fourth Edition

Lynn Russell
Professional Development Company

Mary Munter
Tuck School of Business at Dartmouth College

D0099405

Boston   Columbus   Indianapolis   New York   San Francisco   Upper Saddle River
Amsterdam   Cape Town   Dubai   London   Madrid   Milan   Munich   Paris   Montréal   Toronto
Delhi   Mexico City   São Paulo   Sydney   Hong Kong   Seoul   Singapore   Taipei   Tokyo

Editor in Chief: Stephanie Wall
Acquisitions Editor: Sarah Parker McCabe
Director of Editorial Services: Ashley Santora
Editorial Project Manager: Karin Williams
Editorial Assistant: Ashlee Bradbury
Director of Marketing: Maggie Moylan
Production Project Manager: Clara Bartunek
Creative Director: Jayne Conte
Cover Designer: Karen Salzbach
Manager, Visual Research: Beth Brenzel
Manager, Rights and Permissions: Shannon Barbe

Manager, Cover Visual Research & Permissions: Karen Sanatar
Cover Image: Getty Images
Full-Service Project Management: Saraswathi Muralidhar, PreMediaGlobal
Composition: PreMediaGlobal
Printer/Binder: Edwards Brothers Annex, Inc.
Cover Printer: Lehigh-Phoenix Color/Hagerstown
Text Font: 10.5/12 Times

Microsoft and/or its respective suppliers make no representations about the suitability of the information contained in the documents and related graphics published as part of the services for any purpose. All such documents and related graphics are provided "as is" without warranty of any kind. Microsoft and/or its respective suppliers hereby disclaim all warranties and conditions with regard to this information, including all warranties and conditions of merchantability, whether express, implied or statutory, fitness for a particular purpose, title and non-infringement. In no event shall Microsoft and/or its respective suppliers be liable for any special, indirect or consequential damages or any damages whatsoever resulting from loss of use, data or profits, whether in an action of contract, negligence or other tortious action, arising out of or in connection with the use or performance of information available from the services.

The documents and related graphics contained herein could include technical inaccuracies or typographical errors. Changes are periodically added to the information herein. Microsoft and/or its respective suppliers may make improvements and/or changes in the product(s) and/or the program(s) described herein at any time. Partial screen shots may be viewed in full within the software version specified.

Microsoft® and Windows® are registered trademarks of the Microsoft Corporation in the U.S.A. and other countries. This book is not sponsored or endorsed by or affiliated with the Microsoft Corporation.

Many of the designations by manufacturers and seller to distinguish their products are claimed as trademarks. Where those designations appear in this book, and the publisher was aware of a trademark claim, the designations have been printed in initial caps or all caps.

Library of Congress Cataloging-in-Publication Data
Russell, Lynn.
    Guide to presentations / Lynn Russell, Mary Munter.—4th ed.
        p. cm.—(Pearson "guide to" series in business communication)
    Includes bibliographical references and index.
    ISBN-13: 978-0-13-305836-9
    ISBN-10: 0-13-305836-0
    1. Business presentations.   I. Munter, Mary.   II. Title.
    HF5718.22.M86 2014
    658.4'52—dc23
                                                              2012037973

10 9 8 7 6 5 4 3 2 1

ISBN 10:   0-13-305836-0
ISBN 13: 978-0-13-305836-9

Table of Contents

PART I
PRESENTATION
STRATEGY

CHAPTER 1

ANALYZE THE AUDIENCE   5

Who are they?   6
What do they know and expect?   9
What do they feel?   13
What will persuade them?   15

CHAPTER 2

IDENTIFY YOUR INTENT   25

Consider your general purpose   26
Write your presentation objective   30
Use your objective to stay focused   34

CHAPTER 3

MAKE THE MOST OF THE MESSAGE   37

Make your message memorable   38
Consider the medium   48

PART II
PRESENTATION
IMPLEMENTATION

CHAPTER 4

CRAFT THE CONTENT   55

Explore possible content   56
Decide what to say   62
Prepare for Q&A   69

CHAPTER 5

DESIGN YOUR VISUALS   79

Start with your titles   81
Design a basic template   87
Think visually as you design   100
Edit your efforts   113

CHAPTER 6

REFINE YOUR NONVERBAL DELIVERY   119

Analyze your nonverbal style   120
Practice your delivery   130
Manage your nervous symptoms   136

Introduction

Welcome to the fourth edition of *Guide to Presentations*. We continue to hear from students and executives how much they appreciate the book's conciseness, organization, professional orientation, and readable format—and we are pleased to retain those features in this new edition. At the same time, however, we have updated it significantly.

HOW THIS BOOK CAN HELP YOU

When you are working on a presentation and have specific questions, refer to a page or section of this book for help. For example:

- If you are speaking to a new group of colleagues and wonder how you can come across as credible, start by following the ideas on page 10. Then find the right tools among those listed on pages 20 and 21.
- If you have an important message that needs to stand out and want to know how to make it memorable, refer to the first part of Chapter 3.
- If you are worried that someone is going to ask a question you can't answer, read the section on question and answer sessions, which starts on page 69.
- If you are making a presentation deck, but are more used to making PowerPoint slides, compare their differences with the table on page 80.
- If, like many other people, you feel nervous about presenting, check the tips for managing speech anxiety, which begin on page 136.

On the other hand, maybe you aren't working on a specific talk, but want general guidelines on how to become a better presenter. If so, read through the entire book. By doing so, you will know all the steps involved in preparing and delivering an effective presentation and have an easy-to-skim reference available when it's time to prepare and present your next talk.

WHY THIS BOOK WAS WRITTEN

Between the two of us, we've taught at many colleges and universities, including Stanford, Dartmouth, and Columbia. We've assisted business executives working in an array of industries and other leaders, ranging from directors of community groups to government officials on the other side of the globe. Our students and clients often say they want a resource that is both professional and readable. We have done our best to write a guide that matches those interests by using examples based on real presentations, relying on plain language, and including headings that are easy to skim.

HOW THIS EDITION IS UPDATED

To update and enhance the book, we've made changes to all six chapters. We've also added several pages of web references so you can read, watch, and listen to information that builds on what is in the book. We describe some of the more important changes below.

Changes in Part I: AIM Strategy

- *Analyze the audience.* Our framework for analyzing audiences still relies on four key questions; however, most of this chapter has been rewritten. It includes more detail about emotional appeals, a clearer link between cultural expectations and presentations, and specific tips about how to check your use of jargon.

- *Identify your intent.* We've revised the first two sections of this chapter to make them easier to understand and apply. First, we added more detail about how informative talks differ from persuasive ones. Most importantly, we included examples that illustrate how to master the complex task of identifying what you want your audience to think, feel, or do.

- *Make the most of the message.* In this edition, we put more emphasis on how to use attention-getting techniques so you can keep people's attention on you instead of their tablet or phone. We've added several tables that will help you make good choices about how to structure your talk. We've also updated our list of ideas about to help people remember your important messages.

Changes in Part II: Implementation

- *Craft the content.* This chapter takes you step by step through the process of putting together your talk. Now you will find more ideas about how to use the internet to do your research, several suggestions about how to link information to your audience, and more information about how to use various focusing tools. At the end of this chapter, you'll also find ideas about how to interact with your audience online, using what is called the "backchannel."

- *Design your visuals.* Our focus is on using projected slides and printed decks, but we also include new information about slides that are image-driven (those that rely more on photos and drastically cut text).

- *Refine your nonverbal delivery.* Most of the changes in this chapter deal with tips for helping you practice and manage the nervous symptoms that often accompany a presentation. Specifically, we go into more detail about how to use "Presenter's View," how to rehearse a deck presentation, and how to get ready for talks that are delivered online. To help with speech anxiety, we included more information about how to analyze your symptoms and offer ideas about how to get useful feedback from your colleagues. We also included some new tips, such as "power poses," which you can learn even more about by using the web links in the bibliography.

HOW THIS BOOK IS ORGANIZED

The book is divided into two sections: strategy and implementation.

Part I: Presentation Strategy (Chapters 1–3)

Successful presentations are based on effective strategy. Effective strategy, in turn, is based on three strategic variables: audience, intent, and message. Together, they form what we refer to as "AIM" strategy.

- *Chapter 1: Analyze the Audience.* This chapter explains how to answer the questions: (1) Who are they? (2) What do they know and expect? (3) What do they feel? and (4) What will persuade them?

- *Chapter 2: Identify Your Intent.* This chapter recommends that you (1) consider your general purpose, (2) write a presentation objective, and (3) use this objective to focus as you prepare and present.

- *Chapter 3: Make the Most of the Message.*   This chapter explains how to make your message memorable and why you need to confirm that a presentation is the best way to deliver your message.

Part II: Presentation Implementation (Chapters 4–6)

Part II explains how to apply AIM strategy to three implementation components: content, visuals, and nonverbal delivery.

- *Chapter 4: Craft the Content.*   This chapter takes you through the process of creating your presentation: (1) exploring possible content; (2) deciding what to say in the opening, body, and closing of your talk; and (3) preparing for the audience's questions.
- *Chapter 5: Design Your Visuals.*   This chapter suggests that you (1) start with your titles, (2) design a basic template, (3) think visually as you design, and (4) edit your efforts.
- *Chapter 6: Refine Your Nonverbal Delivery.*   The final aspect of preparing your presentation involves your nonverbal skills—how you look and sound to your audience. This chapter explains how to (1) analyze your nonverbal style, (2) practice your delivery, and (3) manage your nervous symptoms.

ACKNOWLEDGMENTS

LR: Thanks to my coauthor and friend Mary Munter whose work has impressed me from the moment I first read it; to NYU Professor, Irv Schenkler, who suggested important revisions; to Jane Seskin, a great writer and advisor; to Martha Oxenfeldt, an inspiring mentor; to Lucy Ellmann, a witty novelist with an eye for rogue commas; and to Joann Baney, my extraordinary business partner for the last 15 years. I would also like to thank my friend, Aparna Yellai, who worked diligently to improve every page of the previous edition and made many useful contributions to this one, as well as Saraswathi Muralidhar, who skilfully managed this project. Thanks also to my *very* supportive family and friends. And finally, I would like to acknowledge my dad, Bill Russell. I miss his laughter and his love.

MM: I am grateful to the thousands of executives and students I've been privileged to teach; to my colleagues at MCA and ABC; to my coauthor Lynn Russell for her prodigious efforts; and, most of all, to Rob—now and forever (finally!).

We would also like to acknowledge our sources, which are listed on pages 144–149 in the bibliography.

Lynn Russell
Professional Development Company

Mary Munter
Tuck School of Business at Dartmouth College

About the Authors

Lynn Russell has been teaching management communication at Columbia university for over 20 years, first to MBAs and now in executive education programs. She is also the president of a communications consulting company in New York City and routinely assists executives who want help preparing or delivering presentations.

Over the past three decades, Professor Mary Munter has been active in research and teaching management communication, consulted with over 90 corporate clients, and written numerous books and articles. She teaches at Dartmouth's Tuck School of Business and has previously taught at the Stanford Graduate School of Business and various international universities.

Guide to
Presentations

PART I
Strategy Framework

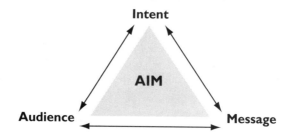

PART I

Presentation Strategy

Y ou face communication challenges every day. Which ones worry you the most? If you ever answer "my next presentation," maybe we can help. Over the years, we have collected some useful presentation tidbits—what to do when your mouth goes dry, how to override PowerPoint defaults, and what not to say as you leave the front of the room. But more importantly, we can tell you the secret behind successful presentations. It explains why some dazzle, while others fizzle; why some are clear, while others are confusing; and why some get results, while others get forgotten.

The secret isn't snazzy. It's just good strategy. The best presenters think strategically. They know the presentation isn't about them. It's about the audience. They realize that if they can't identify how they want to affect their audience, they will struggle to figure out what to say. They accept that competing messages will attract the eyes and enter the ears of the people they want to reach.

Presenters who don't think about strategy are like archers who shut their eyes before shooting arrows. They won't hit the target because they always need to aim. We use the acronym AIM to explain the three connected concepts in Part I of the book:

- **A** = Analyze the Audience (Chapter 1)
- **I** = Identify Your Intent (Chapter 2)
- **M** = Make the Most of the Message (Chapter 3)

You may be tempted to begin by thinking about what you'll say, what slides you'll use, or how you'll look and sound, but be patient; each of these implementation concerns is covered in Part II. Instead, start with strategy. Avoid a presentation misfire by taking the time to AIM.

CHAPTER I OUTLINE

I. WHO ARE THEY?
1. Start with the primary audience.
2. Remember secondary audiences.

II. WHAT DO THEY KNOW AND EXPECT?
1. Consider what they know.
2. Check their expectations.

III. WHAT DO THEY FEEL?
1. Empathize with their emotions and interest.
2. Determine their probable bias.

IV. WHAT WILL PERSUADE THEM?
1. Assess various appeals.
2. Build support with benefit statements.
3. Consider your credibility.
4. Determine how to reach the decision makers.

CHAPTER I

Analyze the Audience

A udiences lose interest when you deliver canned comments. They are pleasantly surprised when they find out what you are saying and how you are saying it has been based on them. However, it takes work to understand the people in the room and the others who will be affected by your talk. You can't just rely on assumptions. Instead, you have to pick up your phone, talk to people, check their internet presence, and attempt to get inside the heads and hearts of your audience members. If you do a good job, you will be able to appreciate how it feels to walk in their shoes.

This chapter gives you a framework to guide your efforts. It is based on four deceptively simple questions: (1) Who are they? (2) What do they know and expect? (3) What do they feel? and (4) What will persuade them?

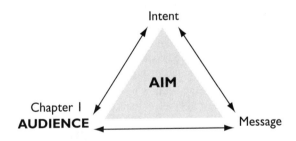

I. WHO ARE THEY?

The first question is the big, broad one. To answer it, collect group data. Then look beyond the categories and focus on the individuals who will be listening to your talk. These listeners are your primary audience. However, they aren't the only ones to consider. Also think about "secondary" audiences—people who will hear about your presentation, or be affected by it, even if they won't be visible on the day you present.

I. Start with the primary audience.

How you analyze an audience depends on the situation. For example, if you are assessing a huge, diverse group, you may want to segment it, so you can compare the needs and interests of various subgroups. On the other hand, if your audience will be a close circle of colleagues, you should be able to focus on the needs and interests of everyone in the group.

When the audience is unknown, get assistance. Locate people who know many of the audience members and act like a detective. Be persistent as you dig for information. Keep learning new things about your audience up to and even on the day of your talk.

- *Get inside information.* When you are an outsider, talk to people who are part of the group. If someone seems helpful, arrange to follow up so you can clarify vague information and sort out conflicting views.

- *Collect group data.* Find out how many people will be attending your talk. Ask about their age range, their educational backgrounds, and the types of jobs they have. Learn what you can about their gender, race, religion, and culture. Discover how well they know each other and what they have in common. Also check whether they have different levels of fluency with the language of the presentation.

- *Segment big audiences.* Make large groups easier to assess by breaking them into subgroups, such as "the researchers," "the sales group," and "the executive team." By thinking about their varying needs and interests, you'll be able to connect with these groups in different ways.

- *Ask about preferences and traits.* Learn what they have liked and disliked about other presentations. Ask for a description of their traits so you will know whether many people in the group tend to be talkative, punctual, informal, and so on.

- *Focus on individuals.* Discover who knows the most about your topic and talk to that person before your presentation. Also learn about the decision makers who can say "yes" to your request.
- *Continue collecting information.* You can keep gathering information about the audience even on the day you present. Meet the people who arrive early, watch for reactions to what you say, and listen carefully to the questions people ask.

When the audience is familiar, don't be complacent. It still takes work to analyze people you know. Begin by focusing on group data and traits. Then, take a critical look at your assumptions. Sometimes what people are saying and doing isn't what they want to be saying or doing. You may need to initiate some conversations or find other ways to uncover their opinions and preferences.

- *Confirm the group data.* If you know the group well, you can figure out most of this information on your own. Nevertheless, gauge the audience's size, either by requesting that people confirm their attendance or by asking the person who's handling logistics about the group's maximum and minimum size.
- *Analyze people's tendencies.* Think about what the audience likes and dislikes and how they typically behave. Do they engage in small talk and enjoy humor or do they tend to be all business? Do they like to challenge ideas or do they need to be encouraged to voice their doubts? Will they ask for details or do they dread minutiae? If you don't know this information, talk to people who do.
- *Use assessment instruments.* If your work group has gone through a training program that used assessment tools—such as the Myers-Briggs Type Indicator (MBTI) or Tracom's Social Styles—keep in mind what you know about people's preferences or styles, especially if you know this information about the decision makers. (To learn more about these assessment instruments, check out the web sites listed on page 146.)
- *Ask about their needs.* Talk to audience members about their current projects. Ask them about the challenges they are facing or issues they would like to see addressed.
- *Consider using an opinion survey.* If you want to learn about their opinions, ask people to fill out a brief questionnaire. Make it anonymous if you're the boss and you want a true assessment of their opinions rather than their best guess about what you want to hear.

2. Remember secondary audiences.

Savvy executives think about how a company's audiences or "stakeholders" overlap. They realize that when they present to different audiences (such as community boards, employees, and investors), some of the listeners might be connected to more than one group. A message meant for one often reaches others.

When you present, your audience will also have blurry boundaries, so use the overlap to your advantage. Ask yourself: (1) "Who else might see or hear the messages in my presentation?" and (2) "Who else might be interested in or affected by my talk?" Your awareness may enable you to reach a decision maker not in the room or build support for your ideas. This awareness may also give you more control over who sees and hears confidential information.

Expand your reach. Your presentation can have a ripple effect if the audience communicates your ideas to others. To encourage this process. . .

- *Ask the audience to share* your ideas with others who might benefit from them. For example, you might ask someone to pass along information to a decision maker who didn't get to attend.

- *Consider those affected by your recommendations*, such as the people who will end up doing the work. They will be more likely to follow your suggestions if you provide them with detailed instructions and let them know the value of what they're being asked to do.

- *Create clear handouts* that will make your points for you; encourage people to take and distribute the materials. If your slides make sense on their own, you might ask whether you can upload them on your organization's intranet. To reach people outside your organization, you might choose to join a site such as slideshare.net.

- *Use social media* to connect with a wider audience. You might record your talk and use your social media connections to let people know where to view it. Or you might encourage people to tweet your new idea.

Limit leaks. If you decide to present sensitive information, make sure you know and trust everyone in the audience. Remember how easy it is for anyone to send a text about what you just said. Also be aware that whatever you print or transmit electronically will be exceptionally hard to protect. If your goal is to ensure confidentiality, you may want to meet with audience members individually.

II. WHAT DO THEY KNOW AND EXPECT?

The second question considers more than the audience's knowledge of the topic. It also explores how comfortable people are with your words, what they know about you, and what expectations they have about how you will present.

1. Consider what they know.

You might be presenting to specialists or novices or maybe your audience has some of both. Before you decide what you want to say, discover as much as you can about what the audience knows.

Deal with mixed backgrounds. With a mixed group, your challenge is keeping the experts engaged without confusing the beginners.

- *Include the experts.* Before the talk, ask the most knowledgeable audience members for suggestions about how to make the material intriguing to beginners. Also find out where they like to get their information. During the talk, encourage these specialists to add their comments or respond to questions linked to their expertise.

- *Point out the knowledge gap.* Let the audience know about the mixed backgrounds. If the audience is large, you might ask those who know a lot about your topic to raise their hand.

- *Prepare background materials.* Send an email with links to helpful articles or sites; consider adding a glossary to your handouts.

Connect with the beginners. If, like many experts, you can't recall being new to the topic, then find a few people who are and discuss it with them. Pay attention to what is confusing. Compare a complicated process to an everyday activity or sketch a picture to show how something works. Encourage the beginners to alert you to the concepts and words they don't understand.

Identify the jargon. Whenever you have audience members from outside your work group, list your lingo before preparing your talk.

- *Acronyms:* Financial people expect to see CAGR, but others might not know it stands for "compound annual growth rate" when they see it on a chart. Similarly, military officers might present with BLUF, but you might not know to put your "bottom line up front."

- *Words specific to your field:* If you aren't an engineer, you may have no idea what a "manometer" does and unless you pay attention to internet marketing, the use of "freemiums" may be new to you.
- *Words with other meanings:* It's easy to perplex people by using common words in a way they aren't expecting. For instance, a word as simple as "bus" will mean something very different to an emergency medical technician than it will to a commuter.

Address second-language issues. A fast-talking delivery style might not be the only thing making it hard for people to follow what you say. Everyday expressions and culturally based content may also pose problems for people who are learning the language.

- *Clarify common idioms.* For example, rather than ask people to "dot their i's and cross their t's," have them check the details.
- *Avoid confusing metaphors.* Unless everyone is a fan of North American–style football, do not describe a pressure-filled, last-chance attempt as "fourth and goal."
- *Check your use of examples and humor.* Jokes featuring puns, stories rooted in culturally based information, and comments delivered with sarcasm may not be understood.

Think about your credibility. Jot down a list of adjectives that people in the audience might use to describe you. If you are having trouble, you haven't been thinking about your credibility. Credibility refers to what the audience knows about you and how they view your competence and character. Each audience member will have a different idea about what makes you credible, which means your credibility will vary from one audience member to another and from one situation to the next. It won't be easy to figure out what others think of you, but you can start with these questions:

- Have all the audience members met me before?
- If not, what different kinds of first impressions might they form?
- What have they read or heard about me?
- What do they know about my education and experience?
- Will they think I'm an expert on this topic?
- In what ways will they consider me to be similar to them?
- What will they believe is motivating me?
- Will they view me more favorably if I discuss conflicting views?

2. Check their expectations.

If you are presenting to colleagues, you might be very aware of the presentation norms in the conference room. At other times, the audience's expectations may be more of a mystery, so you will need to figure them out.

Determining what an audience expects will be especially challenging if you're presenting to people from another culture. By "culture" we mean more than just country: in addition to regional distinctions, culture refers to norms linked to gender, age, ethnicity, and religion, as well as those shared by work groups, organizations, and industries.

Format expectations: Most of the time, your audience will have lots of expectations about your presentation, ranging from how long they think it will last to how formal they expect you to be. Some audiences won't mind if your presentation isn't typical. At other times, people might not be so flexible, which means you'll need to explain why you're doing something unexpected.

- *Timing:* Ask how long your presentation should be, where it fits on the agenda, and when breaks occur. You don't want to prepare a lengthy presentation if your audience expects a 10-minute talk.

- *Visual aids:* Do they expect a printed deck, projected slides, or nothing at all? Maybe you want to use PowerPoint in a nontraditional way, banning bullet points and using lots of photos instead. Your choice might be a welcome relief to people who have grown wary of traditional slides or it may be seen as way too artsy for a technical talk.

- *Formality:* Find out how to address members of the audience, what's appropriate in terms of dress, and whether to use an informal or formal delivery style. You don't want to discover, after the talk, that Martha preferred to be called Dr. Stodt or that your interpretation of "business casual" violated the company's dress code.

- *Content:* If the venture capitalist in your audience recently blogged about the 10 slides he expects to see in any new business pitch, then you may want to structure your material exactly how he wants to see it. Likewise, if your boss uses stories to connect with clients, then you may want to find out whether she expects you to do the same thing.

- *Q&A:* Determine whether questions are typically asked throughout a talk or at the end. Find out how much time to allot for discussion. If the group has a history of posing challenging questions, learn about this tendency so you can prepare.

Cultural challenges: As you analyze cultural expectations, try to avoid stereotypes and focus on cultural norms. Stereotypes imply everyone in a group shares a trait, whereas cultural norms describe behavior—without judgment—and link that behavior to many people in a group. A stereotype would be: "British people are cold." Expressed as a cultural norm, it might be: "Many British people use formal greetings." When you analyze an audience, it's hard not to stereotype, but try to be aware of when and how you are doing it.

Culture and strategy: Here's a small sample of cultural differences that might influence how you AIM.

- *Audience:* Your audience's opinion of you will be influenced by their culture. For instance, some cultures prize wisdom, age, and experience, while others are more impressed with innovation, youth, or risk-taking. Similarly, what people find frightening or persuasive may be linked to their culture.

- *Intent:* The idea that you intend to use time efficiently and focus on results is part of our so-called Western business culture. In other cultures, time is an experience, not a commodity; by focusing on results instead of relationships, you may be totally out of sync with another culture.

- *Message:* What you say and the method you use to say it depends on culture. For example, in some organizations formal presentations are common, while in others face-to-face hallway discussions are the best way to share your views. Similarly, while some organizations mandate putting your bottom line up front, others would be unaccustomed to such directness.

Culture and delivery: Cultural norms determine if you are speaking too quickly or slowly, too loudly or softly, and too much or too little. They even change the meaning of some gestures. Where you should stand might also be influenced by culture. For example, you might be viewed as distant if there is too much space between you and your listeners or you might make people uncomfortable if you get too close and violate their personal space.

Culture and visuals: Whether people first focus on a slide's background or its foreground has been linked to culture. Color, too, has cultural associations. For example, many Wall Street executives link red with bad financial news. Yet just a few blocks away, in New York City's Chinatown, most business owners see red as a joyful color with many positive connotations.

III. WHAT DO THEY FEEL?

No one, not even a statistician, is driven by facts alone, which is why the third question focuses on people's feelings.

1. Empathize with their emotions and interest.

Do you have any idea what keeps audience members up at night or what entices them to try something new? Getting people to open up about their feelings is difficult, especially at work, which means you might have better luck asking for reactions to your topic. If so, find out whether it sparks excitement or generates concern and whether it is more likely to interest the audience or anesthetize the group.

Gauge their emotions. Perhaps your mentor will be in the audience enjoying your talk, while a rival will be sitting nearby, seething with jealousy. No matter what the circumstances, the mix of emotions will affect your talk.

- *Remember the strength of negative emotion.* A well-known article called "Bad Is Stronger Than Good" concluded that negative emotions are far more potent and memorable than positive ones. If you ignore feelings such as anger, frustration, or fear, then you risk being derailed by a powerful force.

- *Guess people's fears.* Even when you see fear on someone's face, you won't be sure of its cause—whether that person fears a blow to the ego or some other painful possibility. Yet, by imagining what audience members might fear, you will be better prepared to deal with an emotion that can sharpen their focus and narrow their views.

- *Build on positive emotions.* Unlike negative feelings, positive ones have a broadening effect. In other words, helping people feel proud of their efforts can motivate them to take on new challenges and stimulating curiosity can make them more receptive to learning.

Assess their interest. You will present differently to a highly engaged group than you will to a bored clock-watching bunch. When interest is high, give people plenty of time to discuss what intrigues them. Maintain their interest and help them remember your message using the techniques we describe in Chapter 3. When interest is mixed or low, take steps to hook the audience's attention (as described on pages 38–40), and use the persuasion tools on pages 15–23 to change their views. Act quickly on any attitude changes that occur as a result of your presentation. Such changes may not be long lasting with this type of audience.

2. Determine their probable bias.

The audience's bias may be a result of their values, attitude toward change, trust in you, or preference for another option. Often it's linked to how your request affects them.

Evaluate your request. To clarify what you're seeking, write a presentation objective, as explained on pages 30–33. Then you'll know exactly what you want from your audience.

- *Simple requests:* Even if you are making a simple request, still point out the value of going along with it. For example, tell people what they'll gain by attending your talk, why altering their opinion will benefit them, or how your suggestion can solve a problem.

- *Major requests:* When you are making more difficult requests, search for ways to make them seem less demanding. You might try one or more of the following ideas. (1) *Simplify their task.* For instance, you might provide a checklist for people to follow. (2) *Recognize their effort.* You might praise them for putting the team first or applaud a recent success. (3) *Point to little successes.* Make a big problem easier to face by sharing "bright spots" as noted on page 17.

Analyze their bias. Use what you know about the audience's emotions and probable reactions to decide whether their bias will be positive, neutral, or negative.

- *Positive or neutral:* In these cases, state your conclusions or recommendations upfront and reinforce their importance. If you want to "inoculate" the audience against other arguments, briefly present and refute the opposing views.

- *Negative:* In this case, use the techniques explained on pages 15–17 to influence their views. In particular, focus on the ask-for-less appeal and try to build off small agreements. If their negative feelings are linked to you, see pages 20–21 for ways to improve your credibility. Also consider meeting with an opinion leader before your talk. If you can turn this person into an ally, then you will have an easier time getting others to agree with your views.

IV. WHAT WILL PERSUADE THEM?

Based on what you've learned about your audience, think about how you can persuade them. To streamline this exceptionally complex topic we will review a few ABCs of persuasion: **A**—assess various appeals; **B**—build support with benefit statements; **C**—consider your credibility; **D**—determine how to reach the decision makers.

1. Assess various appeals.

Before you put together a presentation, list the possible objections your audience may have to your recommendation, product, or cause. Then analyze the various appeals that can help you overcome these concerns. A few common ones include data-driven appeals, benchmarking efforts, consistency reminders, request adjustments, and emotional appeals. To use any of these appeals well, you need to understand why they are compelling *and* figure out how to mitigate their flaws.

Data-driven appeals: People who pride themselves on being logical and results oriented often respond well to data-driven appeals. The effectiveness of these appeals is linked to the quality of the data and the credibility of the presenter.

- *Use reliable data.* The source of the numbers is as critical as the numbers themselves, so be sure to include it on your charts and tables. If you don't know the source, you shouldn't be using the data. When the source is well respected, it should give more merit to your claims.

- *Examine your assumptions.* Acknowledge the limitations of your data and don't make assertions that go beyond the numbers. For example, when forecasting trends, remember that past performance is not a perfect indicator of future results. Similarly, when sharing survey results, examine how the survey was administered and worded before you make conclusions about the findings. For a humorous reminder that correlation is not causation, follow the link on page 146.

- *Portray numbers accurately.* Don't conveniently overlook the numbers that contradict your views or create deceptive-looking charts (such as those that use 3D views or atypical scales). You'll lose credibility if people discover you are distorting the findings. To test your awareness of good chart design, use the link on page 146.

Benchmarking efforts: Corporations have used benchmarking for decades to chart progress or make comparisons. This technique is useful in situations involving change or uncertainty. It requires finding out what others are doing and comparing that information to what your company is doing.

Benchmarking is most effective when you compare your organization or project to ones that are admirable or similar. For example, when looking at "best practices" for campus recruiting, an executive will be most impressed when those practices are used by companies he respects. Similarly, if a governor is trying to decide how much money to budget for disaster preparedness, she may be persuaded to increase the total if she learns other comparably sized states in the region spend much more.

Communication expert JoAnne Yates concludes, "although the fact the 'everyone else is doing it' may not be a very good logical argument, it nevertheless influences some people." For this reason, benchmarking has been labeled "the bandwagon appeal": determine if your comparisons are compelling enough to get your audience to jump on the bandwagon.

Consistency reminders: As persuasion expert Robert Cialdini explains, most people want to be viewed as reliable and consistent. As a result, they often work hard to deliver what they have promised and continue to support efforts they have previously endorsed. In other words, they like to "walk the talk."

There are many ways to use consistency reminders in a presentation. For example, if a CEO has recently praised his organization's values, he will feel the pull of consistency if you can show how your recommendations are linked to those values. Similarly, if you can get your audience to agree "yes, there is a security problem," then they will be more willing to explore solutions to that problem.

Like all other appeals, consistency reminders work better on some people than others. For people who value traditions and tend to resist change, the pull of consistency can be especially persuasive. In such cases, if you position a new idea as part of a continued effort, then you might make an innovation more palatable.

A problem surfaces when people are more interested in new approaches than customary ones. Such individuals might be quick to point out that when circumstances change, their opinions do, too.

Request adjustments: Sometimes you'll want to decrease or expand your request to be more persuasive.

- *Ask for less:* Maybe their concern is "it's just too expensive" or "it will drain other resources." In such cases, consider asking for only a small part of what you really want. For example, suggest a pilot program, recommend a trial purchase, or sign up volunteers for a fact-finding committee. Any of these small steps is a way to get your "foot in the door." Once people have given you an initial commitment, you can use the power of consistency reminders to get them to agree to future appeals.

- *Ask for more:* Sometimes known as the "door-in-the-face" technique, this tactic is the opposite of the previous one. It has you begin by asking for more than you really want. After the audience objects to your overwhelming request, you find out whether they are willing to accept a small part of it. After all, if you are willing to lessen your demands, it seems fair that they should compromise, too. Clearly there is a danger in playing the back-and-forth game of reciprocal concessions; if the audience feels no need to work with you, they may simply slam the door.

Emotional appeals: When used appropriately, emotional appeals can be more persuasive than cold, hard facts. They can reassure, motivate, or inspire a group.

- *Personalize numbers.* Even statistics aren't purely logical. (For instance, people tend to remember findings that reinforce their views better than those that don't.) To help a number resonate with your audience, personalize it—link it to something that affects them. Hans Rosling, a well-known statistician, has a gift for humanizing numbers; you'll find a link to one of his talks on page 146.

- *Include stories with compelling characters.* At times you may want to illustrate your points with more than basic examples; instead, you might tell a story that introduces your audience to an empathetic character as it reinforces your messages. See pages 39 and 58 for more information about stories.

- *Identify "bright spots."* Authors Chip and Dan Heath explain how we can overcome our tendency to get bogged down by a big problem by focusing on little successes or "bright spots." Rather than looking for a big solution to a big problem, they suggest searching for examples of little successes. Highlighting these bright spots sparks optimism, enabling people to feel that even difficult problems can be overcome.

2. Build support with benefit statements.

"WIIFM" stands for "what's in it for me?" It's a question audience members often ask themselves and one you can answer with a benefit statement.

Creating a benefit statement involves three steps. First, you identify all the features of a product or an idea. Next, you think about the audience: the more you know, the better your audience filter will be. Finally, you combine what you know about a feature with what you know about the audience to explain what's in it for them.

Step 1: Identify the features. All products, services, and ideas have many, many features. Features are value-free. They are simply facts about the item or idea you are selling. We'll use this book as an example. Here are some of its features: two authors, six chapters, an index, descriptive headings, a section that addresses speech anxiety, and so on. Some of these features could be turned into a benefit statement for you. Others may have little or no value to you.

Identifying an idea's features tends to be harder than generating features related to a concrete item such as a book. Nevertheless, try to identify the facts behind your ideas. For example, a real estate professional may discover many facts linked to her idea of relocating corporate headquarters. Those facts may include that her plan: (1) affects the commute of 1,000 people, (2) can begin next year, (3) involves buying rather than leasing, (4) proposes a site near a train station, (5) includes space for an on-site gym, and so on.

Step 2: Apply an audience filter. Once you have identified as many features as possible, analyze them from the audience's perspective. You may discover that a feature will actually lead to an objection rather than a benefit. For example, while some people may be thrilled to have an employee gym, others may consider it a frivolous perk. Your understanding of the audience will act like a filter, allowing you to set aside features that won't be useful and identify those important to the group. As you assess features, remember that people have interests beyond WIIFM. Some might want to know how a feature benefits others. More skeptical listeners might want you to admit what's in it for you.

Step 3: Create a benefit statement. Benefit statements address needs and desires. They can relate to something specific such as profits, bonuses, extra space, or useful advice. They may also involve general improvements, saving people time, simplifying a complex task, reducing errors, or boosting morale.

In some cases, simply noting how a feature leads to a general benefit is enough. For example, one feature of this book is its descriptive headings. Their general benefit is that they allow people to skim. Most people realize that skimming can be valuable, so you may not need to offer any other details. Two similar examples appear in the following table.

TURNING A FEATURE INTO A GENERAL GROUP BENEFIT		
Step 1	**Step 2**	**Step 3**
Identify the feature	**Apply an audience filter**	**Create a general benefit statement**
The book includes a **section on speech anxiety**	An audience that includes many nervous presenters	Different techniques work for different people. One of the tips in this section might be the one that helps you sleep better the night before a big presentation.
The plan proposes a **site near a train station**	An audience that includes many frustrated commuters and some people with long commutes	Many employees may be able to commute without cars since the proposed site is within walking distance of a train station.

When you are delivering benefit statements to a group, general ones such as those in the table may be enough. However, at other times, you may need to go the next level, creating a detailed statement that makes it exceptionally clear what's in it for them. The WIIFM focus of benefit statements can be combined with other techniques, such as benchmarking or consistency reminders, to form especially powerful, targeted statements. You can also link these statements to the interests of the decision makers, as we will show you on page 23.

3. Consider your credibility.

Credibility isn't a new concept. Aristotle discussed it thousands of years ago, partially defining it as the combination of a speaker's competence and character. As we explained on page 10, your credibility is based on your audience's perception of you, and this perception varies greatly from one situation to the next.

Based on what the audience knows about you and what you've learned about them, figure out which of the following techniques are appropriate. Be aware that highly interested and motivated audiences are more likely to be swayed by appeals linked to your content than by those related to your credibility. However, for less-interested audiences, credibility appeals may be very important. We've divided these credibility-enhancing tips into two sections: those based on your competence and those linked to your character.

Competence credibility: It's not surprising that if the audience thinks you are competent, they're more likely to accept your opinions. Competence credibility can be associated with everything from the type of information you have on your résumé to the smoothness of your delivery style.

- *Authority:* Sometimes your credibility results from hierarchical power. Having the job of CEO, president, director, or chair may send a signal to some audience members that you deserve their attention because of your role in the organization. Nevertheless, be aware that with some audiences, overemphasizing your authority can backfire. They may tire of hearing that they should accept ideas just because those ideas have been endorsed by the people in charge.

- *Expertise:* Your expertise might be linked to a degree, an accomplishment, or your experience, so be sure they somehow learn that you're a doctor, author, MBA, MPA, or specialist. But expertise is about more than just titles and awards: if you've worked on a project for months, then you may also be viewed as an expert. Likewise, if you've succeeded with other similar projects, then referring to those efforts may bolster your credibility.

- *Associations with experts:* You can also acquire credibility by associating yourself with other people the audience finds competent. Try citing studies done by well-known people at impressive institutions or relating the views of a prominent person. Or, have someone the audience respects introduce you so the audience hears this person's endorsement at the start of your talk.

- *Symbols of competence:* The audience may link certain symbols to expertise or success. For instance, if you use the most up-to-date software and presentation tools, the audience may assume you have a high level of technological expertise. However, be careful when using status symbols to build your credibility. What signifies success to you may not be perceived the same way by others.

- *Delivery skill:* A polished delivery style can lead the audience to view you as competent—even if your topic has nothing to do with presentation skills. See Chapter 6 for tips on delivery style.

Character credibility: Some credibility appeals concentrate on the audience's perception of your character. For example, Cialdini notes that people prefer to say "yes" to people they know and like. Another element of this type of credibility involves reciprocation and fairness, which has been dubbed "goodwill" by credibility experts French and Raven.

- *Similarity or common ground:* Audiences tend to like speakers they find similar—whether that similarity is reflected in shared values, opinions, needs, experiences, style, or background. Therefore, you can enhance your credibility by referring to a shared experience, mentioning common values or needs, using familiar lingo, or meeting the audience's format and cultural expectations.

- *Good news:* Your audience will be more inclined to like you if you are delivering good news. For example, audiences often respond positively to speakers who compliment them. On the other hand, when speakers are associated with bad news or unpleasant situations, their credibility often suffers.

- *Attractiveness:* Interestingly, many audiences link an attractive image to being both likable and competent. In essence, there is a "halo effect" when speakers are good looking or well dressed; it causes people to attribute other positive traits to them. Therefore, keeping the audience's expectations in mind, try to dress appropriately and look your best on the day you present.

- *Goodwill:* People often feel a need to reciprocate if you've done them a favor, lent them a hand, or given them a gift. This pattern involves establishing "goodwill." Goodwill credibility also encompasses trustworthiness. For example, if you offer a balanced evaluation of your proposal, mention opposing views, and acknowledge any potential conflicts of interest, then your audience may see you as fair and trustworthy.

4. Determine how to reach the decision makers.

If you are fortunate, you will already know who has influence with the group. At other times, you will need to identify these people before you can analyze what appeals to them.

Focus on three important roles. When possible, identify the decision makers, opinion leaders, and gatekeepers.

- *Decision makers have direct power or influence.* A decision maker may be easy to spot because he's your boss, potential boss, client, or customer; however, titles alone may not be enough to identify the decision makers. For example, in some cases, decision making may be a group effort and you will want to determine exactly who's on the decision-making team.

- *Opinion leaders shape views indirectly.* Unlike decision makers, opinion leaders don't have the authority to approve your request. What they do have is lots of credibility with the audience and the ability to shape the audience's perception of you and your ideas. Opinion leaders tend to be hard to identify if you are not familiar with the audience. Nevertheless, if you know who they are, keep in mind how and when they might use their influence.

- *Gatekeepers control the flow of information.* If the decision makers are not in the room, you will need to route your message through someone else, known as the gatekeeper. Work with this person to get your message to the people you need to reach.

Consider their needs and preferences. If you know little about these audience members, then ask others about them. Find out about their current challenges and discover what interests them. Analyzing these people will certainly be easier if you've presented to them before. In such cases, think about which of your appeals seemed to impress them and which ones they tended to ignore.

Also recall what they have said about their preferences and analyze the appeals they tend to use. Sometimes people employ techniques that they themselves find compelling. For instance, if your boss frequently wants to find out what your competitors are doing, then she might be a fan of benchmarking. If she spends lots of time asking questions about the column charts on your slides, then data-driven appeals might be a better option.

Create targeted benefit statements. You can target your benefit statements so they deliver clear, specific messages that will resonate with various decision makers. The following table uses the example we referred to when explaining benefit statements—the employee gym—and shows how that feature can be turned into several targeted benefit statements, directed at the decision makers in the audience.

TURNING A FEATURE INTO TARGETED BENEFITS		
Step 1	**Step 2**	**Step 3**
Identify the feature	**Apply a decision-maker filter**	**Create a targeted benefit statement**
The plan includes **a new gym.**	For an **opinion leader** who wants to keep costs under control	The gym's cost can be controlled; we'll actually qualify for lower health-care fees once we provide an on-site fitness facility, which means the gym will pay for itself in three to four years.
	For the **decision maker** not in the audience, who recently spoke about his concern for employees' health and well-being	As the CEO recently said, "finding time for our health and peace of mind makes us better employees"; this gym is just one more example our CEO can mention at the next employee meeting to show what we're doing to ensure the well-being of our greatest resource—our people.
	For a **gatekeeper** who wants to show his support for the decision maker	
	For another **opinion leader** who is also a yoga enthusiast	The gym offers convenience; even the busiest employees will be able to take stress-reducing yoga classes either over the lunch hour or after work.

When you think about the ABCs of persuasion, don't think of them in isolation. Remember that all these factors can work together to overcome objections, build support, enhance your credibility, and convince the decision makers to say "yes" to your request.

CHAPTER 2 OUTLINE

   I. CONSIDER YOUR GENERAL PURPOSE.
- 1. Presenting in tell situations
- 2. Presenting in sell situations
- 3. Communicating in interactive situations

  II. WRITE YOUR PRESENTATION OBJECTIVE.
- 1. Results-oriented and audience-focused
- 2. Specific, measurable, and attainable

 III. USE YOUR OBJECTIVE TO STAY FOCUSED.
- 1. When to write your objective
- 2. How to use your objective

CHAPTER 2

Identify Your Intent

In addition to figuring out what your audience wants and needs, you have to determine what *you* want and need, which is why this chapter helps you identify your intent.

As a presenter, you are attempting to move your audience from where they are to where you want them to be. At first, you may have a vague idea about why you are presenting, but most likely, you won't be able to specify exactly what you are seeking. If you use a focusing tool called a "presentation objective," you'll be able to clarify your goal. You'll also pick up a new skill, one that will make you more focused and efficient whenever you present.

In this chapter, we start by having you think about the general purpose of your talk. Next, we explain how to create a presentation objective. Finally, we let you know how you can use this tool to stay on track as you plan and deliver your talk.

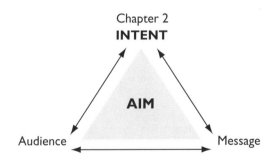

I. CONSIDER YOUR GENERAL PURPOSE.

Before you focus on your presentation objective, step back and think about how you will be communicating to and with your audience.

In a traditional presentation, the speaker takes on the role of expert or advocate and focuses on delivering information to the group. However, sometimes communicators choose to see themselves more as facilitators. In such cases, they focus on encouraging comments or generating ideas *from* the group. One thing that differentiates speakers and facilitators is their level of control.

As speakers, many of us prefer being comfortably in control of a situation. However, we pay a price for that comfort: there's always a trade-off between our control and the audience's involvement. When we have lots of control, there won't be much involvement. To get the audience involved, we need to give up some control. The diagram below shows this trade-off. A specialist sharing her expertise is at the "tell" end of the scale. A facilitator encouraging his audience to generate solutions would be at the other end of the trade-off.

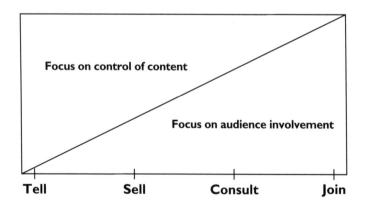

- *Tell:* delivering content *to* inform the audience
- *Sell:* delivering content *to* change the audience's behaviors or views
- *Consult:* seeking questions, comments, and insight *from* the audience
- *Join:* needing new ideas or guidance *from* the audience

I. Presenting in tell situations

If you want to give a progress report, review financial results, welcome new employees, deliver how-to information, or share a customer's experience, you are in a "tell" situation, trying to provide information. Whether your presentation is labeled a project update, a financial analysis, welcoming remarks, a training session, or a customer's story, it is some sort of informative talk. In all these cases, you want people to take in and remember your ideas.

Note the focus on what, how, or who. When you are in a tell situation, you are concerned with information that emphasizes "what," "how," or "who." For example, you might need to talk about what happened last quarter, how a new procedure is done, or who visits a website.

Figure out your general purpose. The general purpose might begin with a verb like one of these: explain, review, inform, update, analyze, point out, compare, or share. Dig a little deeper and you will find the general purpose of your talk. It might be similar to one of these examples:

General purposes that focus on "what"
- Explain the new dividend policy
- Share my vision for the company
- Update the board about community relations activities

General purposes that focus on "how"
- Review the steps of new computer security procedures
- Let investors know how to monitor their portfolios
- Apply several best practices to our campus recruiting

General purposes that focus on "who"
- Analyze the organization's stakeholders
- Introduce new task force members and their roles
- Compare online customers and in-store shoppers

Consider whether you need involvement. Audience involvement is low in a "tell" presentation, but unless your purpose is straightforward, you may discover that the situation isn't just "tell"—that it requires a little bit of "sell." For instance, your general purpose may be to apply best practices to campus recruiting, but you may also want to motivate the seasoned recruiters to assist less-experienced personnel.

2. Presenting in sell situations

When you are pitching a product or trying to change attitudes or behaviors, you're in a "sell" situation. In such cases, you often want your audience to accept your thinking and then do or say something as a result.

Note the focus on why and the link to change. One of the big differences between informative presentations and persuasive ones is the switch from a "what, how, or who" focus to one that emphasizes "why" and pushes for change. When you are selling, you aren't just focusing on how to do something; instead, you're getting people to accept why it needs to be done and energizing them to do it. You don't want people to just remember your ideas; you want them to appreciate why your ideas are important and convince them to agree with you.

Figure out your general purpose. You might start out with a brief phrase (encourage their support or avoid budget cuts). If you add some detail, you'll know the general purpose of your talk. For example, maybe you already know what you want them to support—wind power. Or maybe you know which cuts you want to avoid—those to the research budget. These examples imply a "why" focus—*why* the community would benefit from wind power or *why* senior executives should fund current research. Other examples are listed below:

> *General purposes that focus on "why"*

- Convince executives to relocate corporate headquarters
- Encourage the sales team to use more marketing tools
- Promote the importance of disaster preparedness

Remember that change requires involvement. Usually, when you ask people to change, you will experience some resistance. To overcome it, you will need to involve your audience in some way.

Closing a sale is easier when you can hear and respond to the audience's concerns, which is why many sales talks include time for question and answer (Q&A) sessions. The audience's involvement may sound like a know-it-all analyst questioning your calculation or a sympathetic colleague wondering out loud how to implement your plan. While such questions and comments are a good way to encourage participation, you might need more than rational questions and logical replies. Frequently, to prompt change, you will also have to connect with the audience in an emotional way.

3. Communicating in interactive situations

If you are seeking information *from* the audience, rather than delivering information to them, you are in a "consult" or "join" mode, which means you will be acting more like a facilitator than a presenter.

Consult situations: When you choose to concentrate on the audience's questions and comments rather than prepared remarks, you are transitioning into consult territory.

- *Focusing on questions and answers:* Many presentations include time for Q&A, but sometimes the audience's questions and comments take center stage. For example, at a town hall event, the presenter may begin with some brief remarks, but then quickly open the floor to questions. In this case, the speaker's most obvious role is to listen to the audience's concerns, interests, and questions and to offer on-point replies.

- *Considering your general purpose:* In consult situations, your general purpose will focus on what you want from the audience. Perhaps you want to "get their reactions to the strategic plan" or maybe you want them to "ask questions about the new travel policy." Later, as you clarify your objective, you will also want to identify a few messages you want to emphasize so you can find ways to weave those messages into your replies.

Join situations: When you need ideas and support from the audience, you are in "join" mode. For example, you may need the audience's help in figuring out how to generate ideas or critique options.

- *Choosing to work as a group:* In a "join" situation, you will have very little control. You might begin by briefly explaining how and why you need people's assistance. Next, you might encourage the audience members to generate ideas, making your time together more like a brainstorming meeting than a presentation. Or you might deliver a traditional presentation and follow your talk with small group sessions, asking the audience to supply the information you need.

- *Considering your general purpose:* Focus on what you want the audience to do and view your role as motivating them to do it. For example, your general "join" purpose might be to "identify possible crises that could devastate the organization." To motivate the audience to think about these ideas, you may need to begin by emphasizing the importance of disaster preparedness and follow by having the group discuss and determine the most serious potential crises.

II. WRITE YOUR PRESENTATION OBJECTIVE.

Writing a presentation objective benefits you in many ways. For example, it saves you time by preventing you from researching topics you won't end up mentioning or from making dozens of slides no one will see. It provides clues about how to open and close your talk. And, if some of your presentation time gets cut, it helps you figure out how to adjust.

In this section, we explain how to create a presentation objective that is (1) results-oriented and audience-focused, as well as, (2) specific, measurable, and attainable.

I. Results-oriented and audience-focused

A presentation objective is more than a general statement about your goals or a recap of your presentation's purpose. Instead, it's a statement you create for your own use—one that keeps you on track as you put together and deliver your talk.

Seek results. Your presentation objective will be useful only if it actually saves you time and helps you evaluate your efforts. Similarly, a business presentation will be successful only if it accomplishes real results. Therefore, from the very beginning, link your presentation to the results you want to achieve. To do so, start with this phrase: "As a result of my presentation. . . ."

Focus on the audience. Although it's easier to think about what you want to say than it is to pinpoint what you are seeking from your audience, the bottom line is that the results you seek are linked to the audience; you want your presentation to affect or influence them in some way. So to maintain an audience focus, continue your objective with the words: "the audience will. . . ."

Make changes to the phrase as needed. You can begin with the exact phrase "As a result of my presentation, the audience will . . ." or you can modify it to describe the nature of the talk, as shown below:

"As a result of my sales pitch, the client will . . ."

"As a result of my welcoming remarks, the new employees will . . ."

"As a result of this update, the Board will . . ."

2. Specific, measurable, and attainable

Now, figure out what you want from your audience. To do so, complete the phrase "As a result of this presentation, the audience will . . ." with a list of "targets"—statements that identify what you want the audience to think, feel, or do. These targets should be specific and, when possible, measurable. They should also be attainable as a result of your presentation.

Specify what you want from the audience. Although the words "think," "feel," and "do" sound simple, they aren't. As you will see in the following table, these categories have various, overlapping elements. For example, opinions might refer to something the audience is thinking, but in addition to being fact based, opinions are also feeling based, linked to such things as intuition and values.

SPECIFYING WHAT YOU WANT		
Type of target	**Possible focus**	**Examples**
Think	Knowledge	• Recall two essential tips for safeguarding laptops • Contrast brand awareness by age group
	Opinions	• View research as the top priority • Accept that crisis planning is crucial
Feel	Attitudes	• Be willing to assist less-experienced interviewers • Want to relocate to a convenient, spacious site
	Emotions	• Be proud they achieved the marketing goal • Feel safe because of new security precautions
Do	Mental activities	• Clarify the online information for investors • Adapt our founder's story for clients
	Physical actions	• Applaud the success of our new product launch • Agree to attend two community service events

Consider whether the target is measurable. Measuring feelings may not be possible. Assessing what the audience thinks is often challenging. By comparison, action-based targets will be the easiest to evaluate.

- *Feelings really can't be measured.* You might want people to be proud or feel inspired, yet such emotional states can be hard to define, let alone measure.

- *Opinions are difficult to assess.* To find out people's opinions you could act like a pollster, going around the conference table and asking people to share their views. However, some people might just tell you what they think you want to hear and if the audience is large, such polling wouldn't be feasible.

- *Knowledge is hard to test.* Because you can't use final exams or pop quizzes in the workplace, you will also have a tough time measuring what the audience knows. A trainer may have the time and authority to ask an audience to actually apply or analyze ideas, but you may need to settle for less.

- *Actions are the easiest to measure.* Action-based targets point out what you want the audience to do or say. Such targets make it easy to determine your success.

In addition to *what*, think about *how*. If you link what you are seeking with how you can make it happen or how it might be evaluated, your targets will become more detailed and easier to measure.

- *Figure out how to encourage the feeling.* For example, to build pride, you and your staff could applaud a recent accomplishment; to feel inspired, everyone could listen to a compelling story. Similarly, if you want people to view the new headquarters as desirable, decide which architectural renderings they most need to see. If tapping into an emotion or shaping an attitude is essential, create targets that point out how you can do so.

- *Clarify what you want them to know.* Be careful with words such as "understand" and "know." Specify what they mean. For example, a vague target would be "understand the importance of computer security." By comparison, "recall two tips for safeguarding a laptop" is more useful, especially if it identifies both the tips. To evaluate the success of this target, the presenter might look for nodding heads while suggesting the safeguards and later ask people if they can still remember the advice.

- *Decide how to generate agreement.* Whether you are trying to change an opinion or persuading the decision maker to say "yes," link what you want with how you'll make it happen. For example, what might cause audience members to "view research as the top priority"? Perhaps they need to see the financial risks associated with falling behind the competition or maybe they need to agree to take a tour of the lab. If you can figure out what will be most convincing, you'll know what needs to be a top priority in your presentation.

Choose attainable targets. At this point, you should have a long list of potential targets. It's time to critique them. Think about how they are related. Consider how difficult they will be to achieve. Rank their importance. Whittle the list until it is brief enough to be attainable, yet detailed enough to guide your efforts.

The presentation objectives in the following table use a mix of targets. These objectives include targets that are specific and, in some cases, measurable. More importantly, they worked; each one helped a presenter create and deliver a successful talk.

FROM GENERAL PURPOSES TO PRESENTATION OBJECTIVES	
General purpose	**Presentation objective**
Share my vision for the company	As a result of my presentation, the VPs will… 1. Explain to their direct reports that (a) innovation involves embracing risk and accepting false starts and (b) managing people effectively is both cost-effective and culture-effective. 2. See what I hope our company will look like 10 years from today: an image that features more than two dozen new products on display in our conference rooms and familiar faces throughout the ranks of senior management. 3. Be inspired by anecdotes about the contributions of great managers.
Motivate employees to build off this year's success	As a result of my presentation, the employees will feel proud to be part of a successful team and want to use new tools to achieve even better results next year. More specifically, they will… 1. Give their applause to our six top performers. 2. Find out that we met our goal and expanded market share .24%. 3. Hear three new positioning messages we'll roll out next quarter. 4. Review a list of promotional tools and compare the number available to the number they currently use.

III. USE YOUR OBJECTIVE TO STAY FOCUSED.

Your presentation objective will help you throughout the presentation process—from the early stages when you are thinking about what to say to the final moments when you are closing your talk.

1. When to write your objective

You will be more efficient if you draft your presentation objective before you do all your research. Although audience and intent both need to be considered as soon as possible, different people like to start in different ways. Be flexible in your approach; you may discover that you'll need to modify your presentation objective several times before you determine what you'll say.

Draft your objective early in the process. Many people like to begin with audience analysis and then move to intent, using a system that mirrors the sequence of this book. Others prefer to start with their general purpose, using it as a springboard to collect information and then draft a possible objective. If you are having trouble completing your presentation objective, use a mind map or another tool to help you focus.

- *Using a mind map:* This tool is popular with random thinkers. It can help them generate, focus, and synthesize information. You will find information about mind maps on pages 56 and 57.

- *Trying another focusing technique:* Other tools can help you identify your intent. Several are described on page 59.

Make modifications as needed. Situations change, and your presentation objective may need to be changed, too. For example, you may discover a new computer virus is damaging computers in other parts of the world, so your tips about computer security now need to focus on how to prevent this specific hazard. Or you may learn that people outside the company plan to attend your presentation, so you can no longer include and highlight confidential information. Although the presentation objective is supposed to keep you on track as you determine what you'll say, of course, you'll need to make adjustments as you discover new information.

2. How to use your objective

Your presentation objective keeps you focused as you prepare and present. It also enables you to determine your success.

As you prepare: Keep your objective in mind as you put together your talk. Consider it when you . . .

- *Prepare your opening and closing:* As explained on pages 38 and 41, the first and last parts of your presentation are likely to be remembered; therefore, make sure your opening and closing are linked to your presentation objective in some way.
- *Decide what to highlight:* If your presentation objective identifies a message that you want the audience to hear, use one or more of the attention-getting techniques described on pages 39–40 to ensure the message gets heard.
- *Design your visual aids:* As explained on pages 81–83, your slides, deck pages, or handouts should emphasize what's important, and much of what's important is the information that helps you accomplish your objective. However, don't turn your presentation objective into a visual. It is meant to be a focusing tool, not a slide.

As you rehearse and present: Your presentation objective helps you determine what to cut and what to emphasize. After a timed rehearsal, you may discover you have too much information; if so, a clearly defined presentation objective shows you what to eliminate. Your objective also helps you stay on track when you are answering questions or running overtime. For example, if a question is related to your presentation objective, then you'll want to comment on it thoroughly, making your response of interest to the whole group. On the other hand, if a question is not linked to your objective, then you'll want to address it quickly, but not allow it to sidetrack you from what you are trying to accomplish.

To evaluate your success: You made sure your objective was measurable for a reason: so you can evaluate your efforts. Just because your colleague said, "Hey, you looked good up there!" doesn't mean your presentation was a success. Similarly, a momentary stammer or audiovisual glitch doesn't doom you to presentation failure. Remember, the way you succeed is by setting a good presentation objective and then meeting it.

CHAPTER 3 OUTLINE

  I. MAKE YOUR MESSAGE MEMORABLE.
      1. Hook the audience's attention.
      2. Structure in an engaging way.
      3. Take steps to improve recall.

  II. CONSIDER THE MEDIUM.
      1. Compare presentations to other options.
      2. Use another medium with your presentation.

CHAPTER 3

Make the Most of the Message

Now that we've addressed audience and intent, we'll focus on the third part of AIM: message strategy. Although the term "message" has many meanings, as part of the AIM model, it refers to the content of your presentation: what you include in your talk, how you structure this content, and how you emphasize the points you want to make. It also refers to the "medium" you are using to deliver your content—in this case, a presentation.

The medium influences how information is received by your audience, which is one reason that message strategy is connected to audience strategy. In addition, "message" is very closely linked to "intent." In all cases, your objective should be suited to the medium you are using and it should clearly identify the content you wish to emphasize.

This chapter explains how to make the most of the message. To do so, (1) use techniques to make your content memorable and (2) make sure that a presentation is, in fact, the right medium to use.

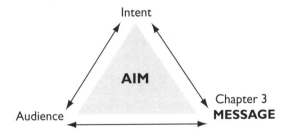

I. MAKE YOUR MESSAGE MEMORABLE.

Much of what you try to remember, you quickly forget. Because what is true for you is also true for your audience, you need to make your message as memorable as possible. This section suggests how to: (1) hook the audience's attention, (2) structure in an engaging way, and (3) take steps to improve recall.

1. Hook the audience's attention.

Not only do you have to worry about how much the audience will forget, but you also have to figure out how to overcome distractions and connect with people who are doing other things. Unfortunately, when it comes to paying attention, multitasking "is a myth," says *Brain Rules'* author John Medina. To make matters worse, as soon as some audience members start texting or talking, others will be more likely to do the same. Given all these challenges, here's what you can do to hook your audience's attention.

Start in a compelling way. In general, something new seems exciting. For example, an opening event—such as a movie premier or the first game of the baseball season—tends to create interest. However, when audience members are not fans of your message, you may need to do something special to get attention as you begin.

- *Include a grabber.* A grabber is something a speaker says or does in the opening moments to attract the ears and eyes of the audience. Good grabbers not only get attention but are also related to the topic. Some are dramatic and take lots of planning. Others are as simple as posing a thought-provoking question. (Page 63 has more details.)

- *Create a favorable impression.* If you explain why you find your topic intriguing, you can convey your enthusiasm for the subject, while giving the audience a reason to find it appealing too.

End with emphasis. Endings don't generate interest the same way beginnings do. Instead of being novel and full of promise, they are reminders that time is running out and one last chance is all that remains. Use these fleeting moments wisely by saying something such as "To wrap up . . ." or "Let me end by saying . . ." Such words call attention to the points you want to reinforce as you end.

Shine a bright light on a key point. By using one or more of the following techniques, you can make a point stand out.

- *Flag a sound bite.* A sound bite is a fresh, crisp comment that captures a big idea. A great one is as rare as a profound tweet. To ensure that a sound bite gets heard, pair it with a "flag"—a signal to listen carefully. (For example, "If you remember nothing else, remember that . . ." or "Here's what's critical . . .") A flag is a pay-attention-to-this signal, reserved for a special point.

- *Craft a relevant story.* Storyteller Sean Buvala often creates his stories from a "float"—a single scrap of information that will register with the audience. (You might find a float by using one of these prompts: "I knew a client who…" or "I remember when…") By adding detail and context to the float, it turns into an anecdote.

  Anecdotes, or little scenes, are the building blocks of a story; they become part of the beginning, middle, or end. Some add sensory details about who, what, why, where, and when. Others might focus on emotions, conflict, or surprise. When they are woven together and polished, they become a story—the retelling of a full experience, one that takes the listener from beginning to end.

- *Create a STAR moment.* A speaker who introduces a little drama can captivate an audience. According to presentation expert Nancy Duarte, if dramatizations are done poorly they can be like bad summer camp skits, but when they are done well they become "STAR" moments or "**S**omething **T**hey'll **A**lways **R**emember."

  Bill Gates once used a well-publicized STAR moment: he made a point about malaria research by releasing mosquitoes into an auditorium. Since you are not Bill Gates, be sure that when you do something unexpected it won't be seen as too gimmicky; otherwise, your STAR moment might damage your credibility and make that damaging moment something they'll always remember.

Analyze what gets attention. Let's examine what made Bill Gates' STAR moment difficult to resist. First, what he did was relevant; the mosquitoes were linked to his message about malaria. Next, he tapped into the audience's emotions and surprised them. In addition, he involved everyone in the auditorium. His actions featured movement and images as well as sound. And they induced tension, until people learned the mosquitoes were harmless. So, to sum up, his moment was **R**elevant, **E**motional, **S**urprising, **I**nclusive, **S**ensory, and **T**ension-inducing. It made every possible distraction easy to RESIST.

Help your audience RESIST distractions. Getting people to stay tuned to your message doesn't always require tons of effort. The table below lists many easy ways to insert attention-getting techniques into a presentation.

HELPING THE AUDIENCE RESIST DISTRACTIONS		
Technique		**Examples**
R	Point out what's **relevant**.	• Flag a key message. • Explain "what's in it for them" throughout your talk. • Offer a solution to a pressing problem.
E	Make an **emotional** connection.	• Share personal information that makes you likable. • Refer to something that makes you laugh. • Use photos or movie clips to capture a feeling.
S	Add an element of **surprise**.	• Include a counterintuitive or shocking statistic. • Make a noticeable change in your delivery style. • Share a fact about your topic that surprised you.
I	Find a way to **include** people.	• Ask people how to solve a relevant problem. • Let the audience choose what you will talk about next. • Get people to talk with someone sitting next to them.
S	Engage their **senses**.	• Add sensory language to examples or sound bites. • Use visuals (or videos) that feature images (and motion). • Bring a prop that people can see, hear, smell, or touch.
T	Create some **tension**.	• Remain silent longer than seems comfortable. • Include a video clip that features conflict. • Make people vote on a controversial issue.

2. Structure in an engaging way.

Now that you know how to hook attention, we can focus on how to hold it by structuring in an engaging way.

Be direct: put conclusions first. The conclusions (or recommendations) count most. They are the big take-away message the audience wants to hear. Usually, you will put them up front, in the opening, while attention is still high. By doing so, you are using a direct approach. It's a structural gift for the audience.

- *A direct approach is easy to follow.* When conclusions come before details, people have an easy time following the message. They don't get bogged down listening to facts about the company or details about the methodology.

- *A direct approach saves time.* Sharing your conclusions first is efficient. If you put your bottom line up front, you can make your points faster.

- *A direct approach focuses on the audience's interest.* Busy executives don't like to wait and wonder when you'll get around to making your recommendations. When you do not give people the information they want right away, you aren't meeting their needs.

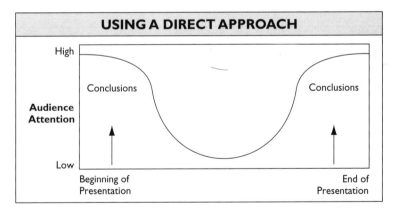

USING A DIRECT APPROACH

High — Conclusions ↑ ... Conclusions ↑

Audience Attention

Low — Beginning of Presentation ... End of Presentation

Reinforce conclusions as you end. The previous diagram shows that attention tends to be high at the beginning and end of a presentation—offering you two good places to deliver important messages. As you can see, with the direct approach, you share your conclusions or recommendations up front and you give them extra emphasis by summarizing them as you end.

If you must, be indirect, by saving the conclusions. When you hold your conclusions until the end, you are using an indirect approach. This approach is like a mystery story; it doesn't reveal the solution until the last minute. Because this approach is harder to follow and more time consuming, we recommend that you use it only when absolutely necessary. You might be forced to choose an indirect approach for one of these reasons:

- *People strongly disagree with you.* Saving your conclusions for the end might keep people from opposing you right away, soften their resistance to an unpopular idea, and convince them you are a fair person, willing to consider other options.

- *Your boss or client insists.* If your boss, client, or other decision makers are exceptionally analytical and want to methodically double-check all your work and assumptions, then you might have to use an indirect approach, no matter how tedious it becomes.

- *You are presenting in another culture.* In some cultures, the direct approach might be viewed as inappropriate or pushy. In these cases, you will want to use an indirect approach to meet cultural expectations.

USING A DIRECT VERSUS INDIRECT APPROACH		
	Direct approach	**Indirect approach**
What to do	Share conclusions in the opening; restate them in the closing.	Save conclusions until the end.
Why do it	• Makes content easy to follow • Appeals to most audiences • Saves time • Emphasizes main point twice	• Prevents disagreements • Makes presenter seem less partial • Appeals to extremely analytical decision makers
When to use it	Whenever possible	• The decision makers insist. • Cultural norms dictate it. • The message is highly controversial and your credibility is low.

Create information chunks. Our working memory—the filter that holds bits of data for about 30 seconds—is quite limited. For a long time, seven was considered the magic number of bits we could recall. But that number might actually be closer to four. This finding does not mean you should stand up, make four points, and then sit down. Instead it explains why you have to find effective ways to categorize information.

If you look at the first line of text in the box below, you'll see a jumble of 12 letters and two symbols that would be difficult to remember. If you look at the second line, you will see the same letters and symbols, packaged in a way that is familiar and much easier to recall. When you chunk information, you boost the capacity of working memory, which is why you want to chunk the content of a presentation.

> ITJO&JYSB&TAMN
> AT&T   SONY   IBM   J&J

- *Create logical categories.* You can find many ways to chunk the content you want to present. Select an option that will make sense to the audience and fit your message.
- *Use a limited number of sections.* Using too many sections can make a presentation hard to follow. Usually, you'll want just two, three, or four.
- *Consider groups of three.* Three is a popular and easy-to-remember option since we can effortlessly repeat a series of three, such as A, B, C; past, present, future; and beginning, middle, ending.
- *Create subcategories.* Complex presentations need to be chunked, not only into main sections, but also into subsections. Be careful: having too many subsections can also make your presentation difficult to follow.
- *Use two-sided options to create contrast.* Contrast can be interesting so you might want to use sections or subsections that consider opposites.

Examples of two-sided categories

Old way → New way

Problem → Solution

Concern → Response

Obstacle → Action

Question → Answer

Drawback → Benefit

Select a structural pattern. Sections and subsections can be arranged in various ways. The most common way is by topic. A topical structure simply lists key points. However, as the following table points out, you can do more than just list your topics. You can even use one type of structure to order your main sections and a different type for subsections.

SELECTING A STRUCTURAL PATTERN		
Pattern	**Description**	**Examples**
Topic	Topical structures are the most common. They limit and list key points or questions.	• Four recommendations • Four essential questions • Three reasons for change • Three research findings
Importance	This option prioritizes topics, arranging them from least important to most crucial or the other way around.	• Range of pressing problems • Priority of crisis responses • Minor to major changes • Rank of departmental goals
Time	A chronological structure highlights "when" by moving from one time frame to another.	• Past, present, and future • The old way to a better way • Past choices, current realities • Checkpoints to our goal
Process	Process structures examine "how" and can often be captured in a diagram.	• Four stages of quality control • Three links between strategy and implementation • Two elements of innovation
Location	A space-based structure focuses on "where." It takes the audience on a tour.	• Touring the new space • Exploring the website • Meeting customer needs in Cairo, Sydney, and Tokyo
Contrast	Although this structure can compare and contrast more than two items, it is often used as a two-sided approach.	• Analysis of our options • A question with two answers • Pros and cons of relocating • Bad news and good news

Solution	This structure starts with a problem, offers a solution, and gives an example of the solution in action.	• Recommendation
		  —Problem it addresses
		  —Solution it would provide
		  —Example of it in action

Explain the flow. Organizing your content into clearly structured sections helps your audience tremendously, but you can do even more to help them follow along.

- *Search for a theme.* Consider whether your main sections imply some sort of theme, such as a formula (showing that $1 + 2 = 3$), a challenge (putting a puzzle together), a journey (looking for several signs), a project (building a strong foundation), or a how-to guide (following the key steps). If you identify an appropriate pattern, you can distill your entire presentation into a simple, memorable theme.

- *Explain the sections in a preview.* A preview is sometimes called an agenda or overview. It lays out the structure you've created for your talk. A preview acts like a roadmap, showing the audience the route you will travel as you deliver information. Previews are important for listeners, because, unlike readers, they can't flip back and see what they missed. Instead they rely on what you tell them about the sections that make up the structure of your talk. See page 63 for some examples of preview statements.

- *Let people know when a new section begins.* When people learn that a new topic is about to begin, they often get more attentive. A new section might not be as novel as the actual beginning of a talk; nevertheless, it is a sign of progress and a chance to reconnect with the message. We explain how to create useful transitions on page 66.

When you use chunking, along with other attention-getting tools, attention isn't as likely to take a nosedive; instead, it will look more like the wavy line shown in the diagram below.

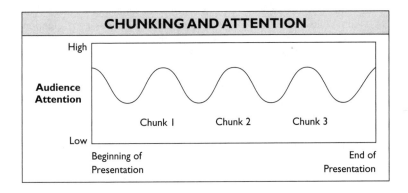

3. Take steps to improve recall.

Memory expert John Medina thinks the most common presentation mistake is "relating too much information, without enough time devoted to connecting the dots. Lots of force feeding, very little digestion." Make sure you don't overwhelm your audience with too much information; instead, take steps to help people connect the dots.

Share the meaning before the details. Beginners and experts process information differently. Beginners struggle to remember details, while experts automatically link those details to the core concepts they already know. You can help everyone process information more effectively if you look for ways to put details in context.

- *Structure for retention.* As we have suggested, use a direct approach and a preview, so the big ideas are up front, the sections are clear, and the supporting details are already linked to the appropriate section.

- *Explain the take-away first.* Share your concept or assertion. Then, go through all the details, examples, anecdotes, and evidence that reinforce or support it.

- *Put clear titles on your visuals.* We call such titles "message titles" and discuss them on pages 84–86. These titles provide the context for all the details that appear on a page or screen.

Show them; don't just tell them. People remember pictures far better than words, so much so that scientists have a name for the phenomenon: PSE or picture superiority effect.

- *Visual + Auditory = Improved Retention.* When people listen to your comments and see an image that reinforces your message, retention improves. Therefore, try to use visuals that feature images instead of words. Use charts, diagrams, and photographs to illustrate your points. However, don't add images that are unrelated to your comments. Needless details, whether pictures or words, will hurt recall.

- *Visuals can show hierarchy.* If the sections of your talk can be shown as a diagram, then people can see, as well as hear, the structure of your talk. However, you can do more than just show your preview on a slide. Presentation expert Cliff Atkinson suggests using different backgrounds to show hierarchy—one for the opening, a variation for main points, and yet another one for supporting details.

Reinforce what needs to be remembered. Showing images on visual aids is one way to help your audience remember essential information, but you also have other options.

- *Repeat what's important.* If a message is important, don't be afraid to say it more than once. For example, if you create a sound bite to emphasize your key message, then you can deliver the statement a second time as you close. Similarly, if your structure is based on a few key points, then you guarantee those points will be emphasized several times throughout your talk.

- *Include some extra examples.* Examples make abstract ideas concrete. They link a concept to something familiar, making that concept much easier to recall. If one of your ideas is exceptionally important, then reinforce it with a few examples; you'll be giving people several ways to latch onto it.

- *Create a mnemonic.* These devices have long been used to help people retain information. Some are rhymes, while others use visual or auditory links to improve memory. One common type, an acronym, makes a word out of the first letters of items in a list. Good acronyms link a simple, relevant word to the message you want people to recall. For example, STAR refers to "**s**omething **t**hey will **a**lways **r**emember," while AIM sums up our approach to strategy: **A**udience, **I**ntent, and **M**essage.

Give people breaks from new information. Whenever possible, stop the endless flow of new information and give people time to reflect on what they've heard.

- *Schedule a break.* It can be a coffee break; a stretch break; or something more high-tech, like a twitter break, where people have time to exchange messages about the presentation.

- *Encourage questions and comments.* Questions don't have to be held until the end; if the audience asks questions during your talk, people can clarify their ideas and make connections. You might include short Q&A interactions after each section so people can process recent information before new ideas get in the way. As another option, you can ask people to discuss a topic with someone else or in a small group before you add new ideas into the mix.

- *Pause.* Silence gives people time to think. Inserting a pause before a key point will draw attention to that point. Pausing again, after the comment, will enable the audience to digest what you said.

II. CONSIDER THE MEDIUM.

If your boss or client tells you that you are giving a presentation, then chances are, you're giving a presentation. In other situations, the decision may be up to you. If so, assess the audience's preferences and decide whether a presentation is the best way to deliver your message.

1. Compare presentations to other options.

Maybe you really shouldn't be preparing a presentation. You can use the following questions to decide whether you should set up a meeting, communicate via technology, or write about your ideas instead.

Should you arrange private conversations? If your audience is small, you may want to schedule a series of individual meetings, which would enable you to stress the importance of confidentiality and deal with everyone's specific concerns. The downside to this alternative is that it will take you more time to get your message delivered, people will hear different versions of the message at different times, and you won't be able to ask for a group decision.

Should you set up a meeting? If you need information from the group and want lots of group interaction, then scheduling a meeting may better suit your needs. Or, perhaps you can deliver a brief presentation as part of an interactive exchange as described on page 29.

Is there a good high-tech alternative? If you and your audience are in different places, you can save time and money by setting up a conference call or by presenting online. However, using technology can add distortions—such as camera angles that make facial expressions hard to see. In some cases, you won't be able to see your audience, which means you won't know how people are reacting to your points, and sometimes the audience won't be able to see you, which means you will lose a powerful, nonverbal part of your message.

Is writing a better option? After you've said something in front of a group, you can't take it back. However, when you write, you can edit your words so they are delivered the way you intended. Writing is also a good choice for complex material that needs to be studied carefully. In addition, it's convenient for the audience; readers get to choose when they want to look at a written message, which might actually be a drawback for you. (You won't know when, or even if, people have received your message.)

What are the pros and cons of presentations? The following table lists several features of a presentation and looks at their benefits and drawbacks.

THE PROS AND CONS OF PRESENTATIONS		
Feature	**Pros**	**Cons**
High control of content or low audience involvement	• Meets your needs when you are an expert or advocate wanting to inform or persuade • Provides control over what content is addressed and how and when it is delivered	• Fails to meet your needs when you want to gather information or work as a team • Limits audience participation, which can lower interest and attention
No record (unless recorded or supplemented with handouts)	• Limits information leaks if the speaker knows and trusts the audience • Can be supplemented with slides or handouts to provide a record	• Makes it hard for people who didn't attend to find out what they missed • Allows information leaks (if the supplemental materials include confidential information)
Face-to-face and group medium (audience and speaker in the same place at the same time)	• Enhances verbal messages with rich nonverbal cues • Enables speaker to make clarifications right away • Allows speaker to seek an immediate response and to measure success based on the presentation objective • Saves time compared to a series of one-to-one meetings • Gets people out of their offices and focused on your message • Offers a chance to build relationships and enhance credibility	• Limits detail (listeners different than readers) • Prevents speaker from avoiding angry audience members • Allows decision makers to say "no" in a public forum, which makes it harder to influence their views later • May involve high costs or scheduling problems • Lacks privacy, making it difficult to deliver sensitive messages • May include poor word choices or delivery mistakes that hurt credibility.

2. Use another medium with your presentation.

If a presentation alone won't accomplish everything you want, then add another medium. For example, you might want to include written materials so you can share detailed information or provide a record of your talk. You might also want to involve the audience by encouraging them to ask questions or express their views. Sometimes it's helpful to think about a presentation as part of a larger effort; you might plan to communicate with your audience either before or after your talk.

Distributing handouts or emailing materials: You can prepare detailed documents or various kinds of PowerPoint materials for the audience to view before, during, or after your talk.

- *Detailed materials:* If you need to discuss complex data, you might distribute a spreadsheet at the point in your presentation when you are discussing those numbers—instead of projecting a table of microscopic type on your slide. You might also distribute articles as background material or provide take-away handouts (such as lists of resources or brochures about your organization).

- *Slideshow emails and handouts:* Some presenters email their slides or print handouts with several slide images on a page. If you pass out printed copies of your slides right before your talk, people might use the images to take notes. However, they might also be tempted to look through the materials when you want them to be listening to you.

- *Presentation decks:* The term "deck" is used in various ways, but as we explain on page 80, we use it to refer to bound printed pages. Decks contain more detail than slides, but they are much less complex than documents. Chapter 5 has information about designing decks; for tips on how to present with them, see pages 133–134.

Including some interaction: Q&A sessions make your presentation more interactive. These sessions can be low-key exchanges or very spirited debates. When you are thinking about what you want to say to your audience, also consider whether you want to include Q&A, and if so, how you want to handle it; see pages 69–76 for more information on how to do so. If you and your audience are comfortable with technology, you might also want to interact online. Pages 76–77 suggest how to communicate using what is known as the "backchannel."

Layering your communication efforts: You may not want to think of a presentation as an isolated event; many times it will be one link in a larger chain of communication. For all sorts of reasons, you might choose to combine several efforts, using one after the other. For example, you might decide that your objective is too complex to be accomplished with a single presentation or you might fear that you're going to face a hostile audience.

- *When the presentation should be the last step:* If you want to make a big change, such as restructuring your organization or moving a company's headquarters, then schedule a series of information-gathering meetings before your presentation; you will want to learn what others think and discuss their concerns before you present.

- *When a presentation is just the first step:* Sometimes, you won't have enough time to accomplish your objective in one presentation. In such cases, consider piggybacking several efforts to achieve the results you're seeking. Consider using follow-up presentations, meetings, or written reports.

- *When the audience has a negative bias:* If you fear you'll be confronted by a hostile audience, then set up private meetings with influential audience members before your talk. Listen carefully to their objections and views. Try to uncover areas of mutual agreement and get a modicum of support before you present to the group; once the group hears that people they respect share some of your views, you'll have an easier time with those who oppose your efforts.

Once you've confirmed that a presentation is, the right medium for your message, you can move from strategy to implementation, as discussed in the second half of the book. However, don't forget to base that implementation on your AIM strategy: **A**udience, **I**ntent, and **M**essage.

PART II

Implementation Framework

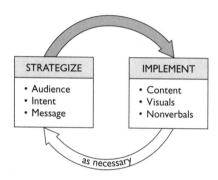

PART II

Presentation Implementation

When most people think about giving a presentation, they tend to focus on the implementation skills we will cover in Part II: What will I say? What will I put on my slides? How will I look and sound? We hope we have persuaded you by now that you should AIM before you start preparing your presentation. Strategy should always drive implementation. For example, your audience should influence your nonverbal delivery; your credibility should affect what you decide to say; and your intent should determine what you choose to put on your slides.

The diagram for Part II, shown on the facing page, illustrates this concept: the dark gray arrow shows how your strategy drives implementation. However, because we don't want to imply that this is a lockstep process (that first you set your strategy, then you implement it), we use the white arrow to remind you to refer back to your strategy, as necessary, while you . . .

- Craft the Content (Chapter 4)
- Design Your Visuals (Chapter 5)
- Refine Your Nonverbal Delivery (Chapter 6)

CHAPTER 4 OUTLINE

   I. EXPLORE POSSIBLE CONTENT.
      1. Collect information and generate ideas.
      2. Focus and order the information.

  II. DECIDE WHAT TO SAY.
      1. Decide how you'll open.
      2. Plan a well-organized body.
      3. Determine how you'll close.

 III. PREPARE FOR Q&A.
      1. Get ready for their questions.
      2. Refine your listening skills.
      3. Respond effectively.
      4. Listen for challenging questions.
      5. Control difficult or hostile audience members.
      6. Deal with online comments.

CHAPTER 4

Craft the Content

Your presentation strategy (AIM) should guide you as you craft the content of your talk. This chapter encourages you to keep strategy in mind as you: (1) explore possible content; (2) decide what to say during the opening, body, and closing of your talk; and (3) think about how you will respond to the audience's questions and comments.

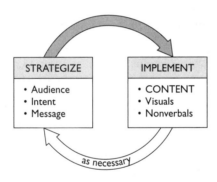

I. EXPLORE POSSIBLE CONTENT.

A good presentation needs good content. Getting that content requires an expert's command of the subject and a talent for generating interesting ideas. It also requires focusing those ideas and arranging them into an easy-to-follow structure.

1. Collect information and generate ideas.

Start by figuring out what you already know. Then research to learn more. When possible, find new ways to express other people's ideas and create content that is yours alone.

Determine what you already know. Often, you will know a good bit about your audience and the topic. But even when the audience is unfamiliar and the topic is new, chances are you'll have at least some awareness of the situation and the subject.

- *Start with strategy.* List what you know about your audience, using the audience analysis questions outlined in Chapter 1. If you are already a subject matter expert, you may be ready to draft your presentation objective as described in Chapter 2. However, if you still have lots to learn, then focus on your general purpose and your audience as you explore possible content.

- *Do a data dump.* Jot down what you know about your topic and identify some of the resources you want to consult. Round up the data, images, and files you need to reexamine. Consider what you know about conflicting views. Make notes about your ideas and the ideas of others that will guide your approach.

- *Try a mind map.* A mind map can help you collect, focus, and order all at once. This technique has you (1) write your general purpose in the middle of a large sheet of paper and circle it; (2) draw branches from the circle to show your main points; (3) label those branches with a single word, a brief phrase, or an image; (4) add secondary branches off the main ones. You'll find an example of a mind map on the next page. To learn more, read Tony Buzon's book, which is listed in the bibliography, or go to buzonthink.com to see more examples. Many software programs enable you to make mind maps on your laptop or tablet. Several are free (such as XMind, MindMeister, and FreeMind). However, if you are using a mind map to determine what you know, you may find you have more flexibility if you draw it by hand.

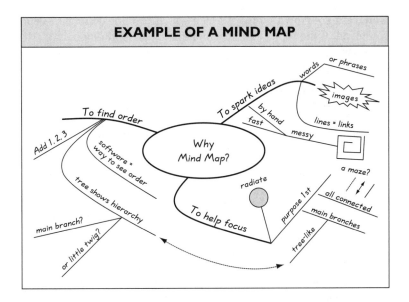

EXAMPLE OF A MIND MAP

Research to learn more. You may need to learn more about your strategy and content. For your strategy, you might connect with people in the audience or check out company websites. To research content, you might work with colleagues who can help you collect and interpret data or you might work alone—studying spreadsheets or surfing the internet. Here are some tips to make your internet searches more effective.

- *How to navigate the internet:* For some good tips on how to navigate, see http://www.lib.berkeley.edu/TeachingLib/Guides/Internet/FindInfo.html.

- *How to go beyond Google:* In addition to just searching on Google, try the advanced searches available on Yahoo Finance or Google Finance. Other free sources include: http://investing.businessweek.com/research/company/overview/overview.asp and http://online.wsj.com/mdc/public/page/marketsdata.html.

- *How to go beyond Wikipedia:* Consider sources such as data.gov, worldbank.org, federalreserve.gov/econresdata (Federal Reserve), nber.org/data (National Bureau of Economic Research), and Investopedia.

- *How to evaluate sources:* As you know, anyone can write anything he or she wants on the internet, without vetting of any sort. Especially when you are using a blog or website, do additional searches to assess the source's reputation.

Generate your own content. Once you are comfortable with your command of the topic, stop researching. You can do more, later, if necessary. Instead, find ways to connect what you know about the topic to what you know about your strategy.

- *Link information to the audience.* Decide what will be new and interesting. (What might get people's attention? How could an idea be turned into a benefit statement?) Review what you know about the audience's possible objections. (What data can address these concerns? Which sources will be most respected?)

- *Synthesize ideas.* Blend several approaches and come up with something new—an idea that is unusual, easier to explain, or more relevant for your audience. For instance, on page 39, we connected one of Bill Gates' dramatic presentation moments to our list of attention-getting techniques.

- *Explore topics for stories.* Storyteller and author Annette Simmons believes most of us can create stories that will interest others. To discover a possible story, she suggests thinking about your past successes, some lessons learned, someone you admire, or a well-known source—such as a book, movie, or current event. Simmons also identifies different types of stories. For example, those she calls "Who-am-I Stories" can build credibility. Those termed "Teaching Stories" can be far more memorable than just giving advice. And her "I-Know-What-You-Are-Thinking-Stories" can be used to overcome an audience's secret objection.

- *Consider solution-based scenarios.* Try to weave a benefit statement into a problem-solving anecdote, a little scene that will resonate with people in the audience. Here's an example of how a benefit listed on page 18 could be linked to several complications and solutions, all leading back to the benefit statement.

    Example of a solution-based scenario

    "Imagine you're stuck in traffic, attempting to turn onto Route 13. What does it usually take? About 15 minutes? Once we relocate our headquarters, that wait will be a thing of the past. For almost 80% of you, the train may be a better way to commute. I realize that some people who live near train stations actually need their cars during the workday—to meet clients or run errands—which is why we're planning to make a fleet of electric cars available in the adjacent garage. But what about those of you who don't live near the train stations? Since the new site has three different access roads—which, unlike Route 13, are all well maintained—your arrival at work won't include a daily traffic jam."

2. Focus and order the information.

At some point, you need to stop discovering possible content and start exploring how the appropriate content can be turned into your presentation.

Draft a presentation objective: Chapter 2 explains how to write a presentation objective. If you haven't done so already, now is the time to complete that task. If you are stuck, do as much as you can. For example, just identify one thing you want your audience to think, feel, or do. Even if you haven't finished your objective, at least you'll have some idea about what you are trying to accomplish.

Try other focusing techniques. In addition to mind maps, there are other focusing tools you can use to help you complete your presentation objective.

- *Nutshell the information.* Writing expert Linda Flower suggests trying to capture the essence of what you want to say in a few short sentences—or to use her words, in a "nutshell." You might also try capturing what you want from your audience in a nutshell.
- *Try the email technique.* Build on the nutshell idea by writing an imaginary email. Assume you are explaining the gist of your talk to someone who can't attend. Focus on this person as you write. What do you want this person to think? What might you ask this person to do?
- *Teach your ideas.* Some people prefer talking to writing. They have an easier time clarifying their ideas if they have a live audience. To teach your ideas, sit with a colleague and talk about your presentation. Explain why it is important, what's interesting about the topic, and what problems it addresses. Ask how the person's thoughts and views changed after hearing about your presentation. Is that the change you are seeking?
- *Try the elevator pitch.* Imagine you have the decision maker's attention for just 90 seconds—the time it would take for a short elevator ride. Pitch your idea. What's it about? Why is it interesting? What makes it worth exploring? Finally, as the elevator doors open, what will you ask of the decision maker?
- *Circle back to research.* If you are still stuck, go back and do more research. Maybe you'll stumble across an idea that will lead to an "ah ha" moment. From there, you might be ready to specify what you want the audience to think, feel, or do and have a good idea about how you'll accomplish those results.

Order the content. Once you've identified the relevant information, you can try to organize it into chunks or sections as described on pages 43–45. Use the following tools to help you discover possible categories and how they are linked.

- *Using an outline:* If you think in a very linear fashion and if you can easily distinguish major themes from secondary points, then you will probably prefer to organize your ideas with an outline: either a traditional one (using Roman numerals and capital letters) or an informal one (using bullet points and dashes).

- *Making an idea chart:* Idea charts are more visual than outlines. To create one, (1) list your important ideas, (2) find ways to group them into a limited number of categories, and (3) label each group. If constructed like a pyramid, your main idea will be in a box at the top of the pyramid, with your main sections placed below it, as illustrated on the next page. For more information, refer to Barbara Minto's book in the bibliography on page 145.

- *Starting with a storyboard:* This ordering method may also prove useful for visual thinkers. To create a storyboard, (1) start with a series of blank boxes; (2) sketch images that capture your ideas in various boxes; (3) write important messages as headlines, or write the headlines first and then sketch the pictures; (4) search for a logical way to group and sequence the images; and (5) number the boxes to show the order. Create your storyboard with pencil and paper, not in PowerPoint, where you may waste time perfecting slides that you later decide to delete. Visualization expert Dan Roam thinks all messages can be shown as pictures. His website, www.danroam.com, demonstrates how.

- *Using your own method:* If these suggestions don't seem helpful, then find a method that works for you. For example, you might try using a combination of mind mapping and sticky notes. Aided by these tools, you could use the mind map to identify important ideas and then transfer them to sticky notes. The notes could then be moved around until they form an idea chart that shows how to order your talk.

IDEA CHART EXAMPLE

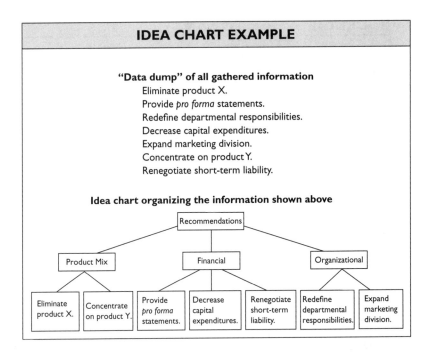

"Data dump" of all gathered information
Eliminate product X.
Provide *pro forma* statements.
Redefine departmental responsibilities.
Decrease capital expenditures.
Expand marketing division.
Concentrate on product Y.
Renegotiate short-term liability.

Idea chart organizing the information shown above

STORYBOARD EXAMPLE

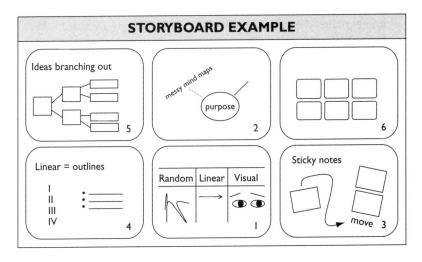

II. DECIDE WHAT TO SAY.

Now that you've gathered, focused, and ordered the information, it's time to turn it into a presentation. In this section, we'll explain how to decide what you'll actually say in each part of your talk.

In one way, a presentation is like a written document. Both have three parts: the opening, the body, and the closing. But, unlike a written document, a presentation needs a structure that is repetitive and exceptionally clear. Listeners aren't like readers: they can't glance back to refresh their memories or skip ahead to check out the end. So when you are giving a presentation, always include a preview that outlines the sections you plan to cover and use explicit transitions that remind your listeners about what you just covered and what you plan to talk about next.

Prepare the opening, body, and closing in any sequence that works for you. Some people like to start with the body and their preview to ensure a clear structure. Others prefer to use a chronological approach—first deciding how to open, then preparing the body, and finally determining how to close.

1. Decide how you'll open.

Your opening is crucial. It sets the stage, builds interest in your topic, and explains the structure of your talk. Although there are several tasks to accomplish with the opening, don't make this section too long or complex; be sure you get to your preview well before the audience wonders where you are headed with your talk.

Set the stage. Use the opening to connect with your audience and introduce the scope of your presentation. For instance, you may use the opening moments to explain your position and how it shapes the way you'll be approaching your presentation. Or perhaps you'll borrow a screenwriting approach: establish the current situation as a dilemma, let the audience know their role, and promise to show them how to achieve a good ending. If you are unknown to anyone in the audience, you will also need to introduce yourself so you can establish some credibility.

Grab their attention. As we mentioned on page 38, when people are focused on something other than your presentation, you can get their attention by using a grabber.

- *Common ways to get attention:* You can ask the audience a question, make a promise about what your presentation will deliver, describe a vivid image, share an anecdote, or explain why the audience should care, perhaps telling them exactly what's in it for them.

- *Techniques to use carefully:* Humor can easily grab attention, but make sure it fits your personality. Like all other attention-getting techniques, humor needs to be appropriate for the audience and related to the situation. You also want to make sure it won't make anyone in your audience feel picked on or left out. In addition, be careful with grabbers that don't actually grab much attention—like long dictionary definitions read off a slide.

Always include a preview. An essential part of your opening is the preview. It provides the structural map of what you will be saying or, in other words, it tells them what you're going to tell them. It's also a good place to let people know how long you plan to speak.

- *Explain the structure.* If you are following a direct approach, which we recommended on pages 41–42, make your conclusions obvious when you give the preview. If you are using a less common, indirect approach, you still need to make the structure clear; however, you will save your main conclusion for the end.

  Example of a preview statement using a direct approach

  In the time remaining this morning, I want to explain the benefits of the new system. First, I'll demonstrate how these new guidelines will save you time. Second, I'll point out how you can use them to respond to client's billing questions. And finally, I'll explain how they address a complaint many of you had about the old system.

  Example of a preview statement using an indirect approach

  In the next 30 minutes I want to discuss two topics. First, I'll describe the record-keeping problems that have plagued our billing system. Second, I'll share three options we have in dealing with them.

- *Show them while you tell them.* Feature your preview on a slide or deck page. When you deliver your preview statement, take your time. Direct the audience's attention to the visual so they can see and hear your message.

2. Plan a well-organized body.

As we pointed out in Chapter 3, your points can't be randomly delivered; they need to be packaged into a limited number of sections. Once you've organized the body of your talk, you can work on your transitions—how you will wrap up one section and introduce what comes next.

For tell presentations: Many informative talks use topical structures. They might list the key ideas people need to remember or the major findings of a research project. However, you can do more than just list topics. For example, steps can be arranged by sequence and items can be compared. The examples below show several ways to structure informative talks.

- *Topical structure:* Suppose a financial executive has identified three reasons the company's new dividend policy makes sense. To make sure the analysts hear that rationale, she might explain the change by highlighting those reasons: (1) investor attitude moved toward a yield preference, (2) surplus capital made the former payout ratio impractical, (3) tax code changes made the new policy more desirable. In this example, the three topics are investor attitude, surplus capital, and tax code changes.

- *Time-based structure:* Suppose a CEO wants to review what the company has done and will continue to do to forge better community relationships. He might update the board by ordering his comments like this: (1) Previously, we participated in local events to raise the company's profile and build relationships; (2) Currently, we continue attending events, while working to solve zoning issues with people in the neighborhood; (3) Next, we will create more public space for the community. The activities are arranged by time: past, present, and future.

- *Contrast-based structure.* Suppose a marketing analyst has been asked to report on customers' habits and preferences and her research shows great differences between the online customers and the people shopping in stores. She can emphasize those differences in various ways. For example, her presentation might list the topics in a way that accentuates specific differences: (1) demographic profile—online versus store; (2) purchasing habits—online versus store; (3) brand awareness—online versus store. On the other hand, she might show the contrast with a two-part structure: (1) a tale about online customers and (2) stories from our stores. Both structures feature contrast, though they do so in different ways.

For sell presentations: As we mentioned, persuasive presentations focus on "why" and push for change. Many use topical structures. For example, they might list the benefits of a product or the reasons to support a change. Yet, once again, the sections can be arranged in different ways.

- *Topical structure:* Suppose employees were asked to suggest ways to improve the ratings for a resort hotel. Although they generated dozens of recommendations, they grouped the most relevant ones into a manageable number of themes: (1) listening to our guests, (2) providing service as a team, (3) creating a sense of luxury, and (4) enhancing our reputation. In each section, they have two or three specific recommendations. For each one, they draw attention to a current or potential problem, explain how the recommendation would solve the problem, and give an example demonstrating the solution in action. The sections of this presentation are topical, while the subsections use a solution-based structure.

- *Importance-based structure:* Suppose the CEO of an alternative energy company wants to convince people in an economically distressed community to let his company build wind turbines. Because he knows some of his points will be viewed as more important than others, he prioritizes them: (1) provides high-paying jobs to people in the community; (2) makes financial sense because of government subsidies; (3) generates quiet, safe, carbon-free energy. These topics are ordered by their importance to the audience.

- *Space-based structure:* Suppose a real estate executive wants to convince a corporate team that she can find them great office space. To get the business, she pitches two potential properties: (1) the Bentley Building, which offers downtown luxury and (2) Georgian Towers, which offers midtown convenience. For each site, the audience sees and hears why the building, the public spaces, and the private spaces would suit their needs. In this example, both the sections and subsections are structured by location.

- *Problem/solutions structure:* Suppose an IT director needs more resources. His proposal is costly and unpopular. The decision maker is exceptionally analytical. Therefore, he chooses an indirect approach, which means he'll save his main conclusion for the end. He also selects a problem/solution structure: (1) cyber-security issues and (2) three approaches that heighten security. His preferred solution comes last. This structure allows people to agree there is a problem before the presenter addresses possible ways to solve it.

Moving from one section to the next: No matter what type of pattern you use to order the body, you need to include clear transitions that reinforce this pattern.

- *Use explicit transitions.* Avoid vague segues such as "second" or "finally." Use detailed ones instead: "A second benefit of wind power involves financing . . ."

- *Take a look backward.* Before you rush to introduce your next point, remind people of the section you just finished. For example, "The economic boost provided by high-paying, local jobs isn't the only reason to support wind power; a second benefit. . . ."

- *Use "backward-look/forward-look" transitions.* If you use explicit language and link the previous section to what comes next, you will create a clear and helpful segue—a "backward-look/forward-look transition." Although you may feel as if you are being too repetitive, your listeners will appreciate these detailed reminders. They will help daydreamers get back on track and alert attentive listeners that something new is coming up next.

USING TRANSITIONS THAT LOOK BACKWARD AND FORWARD

The backward look	The forward look
"Now that I've highlighted the financial incentives...	I'll tell you why wind turbines are quieter than you may think and how this energy compares to other sources."
"So it's clear why we need to do a better job listening to our guests...	But we also need to change the way we work, which gets us to the second set of recommendations..."

3. Determine how you'll close.

Your audience is likely to remember your last words. Therefore, your closing should be more than just "thank you" or the all-too-common "no more questions . . . well then, that's it." Although you always want to avoid such "dribble" endings, your closing comments can take many forms. We'll give you a few ideas about how to end and alert you to the problem of closing your talk after someone has asked a question.

To deliver your closing words effectively, pause and breathe before you say them. Once you have finished, wait a few seconds before heading back to your chair. For more insight about how to use your nonverbal behavior to emphasize a message, refer to Chapter 6.

Closing an informative talk: In an information-sharing (or "tell") presentation, use the final moments to recap what you've told them. In most cases, your presentation objective will remind you what is most important and suggest how to close. For example, your last statement may simply be a sound bite from your presentation objective, or it may be a polished version of how you previously described your presentation using the nutshell technique, which we explained on page 59. Just make sure there is some connection between how you close and what you're trying to accomplish.

Closing a persuasive talk: In a persuasive (or "sell") presentation, your final comments need to close the sale. Use your presentation objective to help you decide how to craft your closing; try to end in a way that will enable you to measure your presentation's success. For example, you might wrap up by . . .

- *Asking the decision makers* for an order or by requesting authorization to implement your recommendations.
- *Distributing a sign-up sheet* so you can collect the names of people willing to volunteer for your campaign.
- *Restating your most persuasive point* and then arranging to talk privately with the decision maker so you can close the sale during this informal conversation.
- *Going around the conference table* and asking people where they stand on making your suggested change.

Using both initial and final closing statements: If you are planning a Q&A session at the end of your presentation, then you will need two closings. The first one will wrap up your prepared comments and segue into a request for questions. Ideally, the second one will synthesize several pertinent moments from the Q&A session and link them to your presentation objective. If none of the questions can be tied to your objective, then your final closing will be a strong, clear statement, similar to your initial closing. Always make sure the final words the audience hears are yours and that they are linked to your presentation objective.

SAMPLE INFORMATIVE PRESENTATION	
Opening	Introduction of presenter and topic Main conclusions Preview
Body	Point 1 (followed by a backward-look/forward-look transition) Point 2 (followed by a backward-look/forward-look transition) Point 3 (followed by a backward look and segue to closing)
Closing	Summary of points/concluding statement

SAMPLE PERSUASIVE PRESENTATION (FOLLOWED BY Q&A SESSION)	
Opening	Introduction of presenter and topic Recommendation Preview
Body	Benefit 1 (followed by a backward-look/forward-look transition) Benefit 2 (followed by a backward-look/forward-look transition) Benefit 3 (followed by a backward look and segue to closing)
Closing	Initial closing (including a request for questions) Q&A session Final closing (featuring a call for action)

III. PREPARE FOR Q&A.

Don't just prepare for the time you'll be speaking; also think about the interactive moments when the audience will be asking questions.

1. Get ready for their questions.

Decide when to take questions and adopt the right attitude, one that welcomes the audience's participation. Also set aside time to rehearse so you'll be ready to answer whatever people ask.

Decide when to take questions. You can take questions at the end of the talk or have people ask them throughout. Find out what the audience expects and think about what you prefer.

- *Holding questions for the end:* Ending with questions gives you control of the schedule and flow of information. However, there are risks with this choice: (1) people might be confused if they can't ask questions in the moment and (2) you might find yourself in an awkward situation if people ask questions after you've asked them not to do so.

- *Taking questions throughout:* If people can ask questions during your talk, they can get clarification when they need it. Having interactive moments in the middle of your presentation may also help the audience listen more attentively. However, questions can also upset your schedule and take you off point. To minimize these drawbacks, (1) budget time for questions instead of planning to speak for the entire time you've been allotted and (2) control digressions by using the listening and responding skills described on the following pages.

Value questions. When someone asks a question or shares a comment, think of it as a compliment—"my audience is interested enough to want a little more detail"—or as a bit of useful information—"now I know my client's views." Adopting this attitude will help you create the right tone for Q&A.

Practice responding. Anticipate what the audience will ask and practice a few different responses. Have someone help you by posing common questions such as those related to cost, timing, alternatives, and risks. Also ask this person to challenge you with unexpected questions or negative comments. If you can record this rehearsal, you will get useful information about how you listen and respond.

2. Refine your listening skills.

Listening expert Robert Bolton breaks listening skills into three clusters of behavior. Use these skills to (1) look like a good listener, (2) encourage participation, and (3) paraphrase the questions you are asked.

Look like a good listener. Use various nonverbal behaviors to show your audience you are interested in their questions. Check your posture, movement, and eye contact to make sure you appear attentive. Also make sure the atmosphere is right for Q&A.

- *Maintain a posture of involvement.* Face the questioner. Avoid distracting hand or arm placements such as resting your chin on your hand or crossing your arms in front of your chest. Hold your body still: stop any needless movements, such as tapping your feet, clicking a pen, or fidgeting with your notes. Let your body language signal that you're listening intently.

- *Make eye contact.* Look at the questioner, observing her whole face so that you can pick up nonverbal cues.

- *Create an environment suitable for listening.* If appropriate, consider moving to the side of the podium or in front of a table, closing the distance between you and the audience. During Q&A, turn up the lights so the audience can be the focus of your attention.

Encourage participation. Get people to participate by posing open-ended questions, being silent, and using small signals that encourage them to continue talking.

- *Open the door for questions.* Use open-ended questions that can't just be answered "yes" or "no." Rather than begin with the words "Can you" or "Do you," start with phrases such as "What's your view of" or "Tell me about."

- *Be silent: don't interrupt.* After you've asked a question or invited people to participate in a Q&A session, give them time to think. Wait patiently for at least 10 to 15 seconds so people can collect their thoughts. Don't say anything while you wait. Also, be silent as you listen to their questions. If you interrupt, you won't hear the entire question, and you'll send a signal that you're rushing them.

- *Use minimal encouragers.* Also consider using little cues, called "minimal encouragers," which entice a speaker to continue: nodding, smiling, tilting your head, widening your eyes, or saying "uh huh." As long as these signals are natural, they communicate that you are genuinely interested in listening to the question.

Paraphrase the question. In active listening, a paraphrase is a brief statement that captures the essence of what someone just said. It's a statement that helps people feel heard and one that can prevent miscommunication. If modified a bit, this listening tool can be a great asset when handling questions.

Like regular paraphrasing, Q&A paraphrasing involves more than just repeating what someone said. Instead, a paraphrase translates an audience member's words into your own. Both types are brief, but regular paraphrasing focuses on helping the other person, whereas Q&A paraphrasing is used to help you control the interaction and enhance the value of Q&A for everyone in the room.

- *Keep everyone involved:* If someone sitting in the front row asks a question, people sitting in the back may not be able to hear it. Therefore, you need to repeat the question, or better yet, paraphrase it. By doing so, you make sure everyone knows what was asked.

- *Clarify what was asked:* Questions can be hard to understand for many reasons. Maybe the questioner used vague words and created such a long question that you don't know where to begin. Or maybe the question itself was phrased in a way that it seems to be controlling how you can respond. In these situations, a paraphrase can help you deal with the question. Pages 73–74 offer examples of challenging questions that need to be paraphrased.

- *Address emotions:* Some questioners let you know how they feel; for example, they may directly state that they are "confused," "delighted," or "extremely worried." Others use only visual and vocal cues to express their feelings. Never forget that these nonverbal cues are part of the question. For example, maybe one questioner's face shows his frustration, while another questioner expresses her irritation with a sarcastic vocal tone. In such cases, you want to paraphrase more than just the actual words. When feelings trump the facts, you might paraphrase by saying something like this: "I recognize that many of you are extremely frustrated by the new paperwork requirements, so let's get to the root of Pat's question: Why do we need to replace a simple, one-page form with this new detailed one?"

- *Diffuse difficult situations:* When you need time to think, paraphrasing can be a great stalling technique. It gives you a chance to gather your thoughts before you respond. Paraphrasing is also a handy weapon in your arsenal if you are battling hostile questioners. For more information about these difficult interactions, see pages 75–76.

3. Respond effectively.

Effective responses help you accomplish your objective. Ideally, they should also be interesting and delivered in a way that keeps your audience involved.

Stay on message. When you are asked a question, think of it as a chance to make your message heard. To do so, use two powerful techniques: "bridging" and "flagging."

- *Bridging* connects your response to something that is part of your presentation objective. A bridge can be a connecting phrase, such as "which means," or a simple word, such as "and." For example, a bridge might sound like this: "Karla, you've asked an important question about wildlife safety, so I'll address the potential hazards you mentioned *and* explain how we protect birds, animals and plant life at our facilities."

- *Flagging* draws attention to your most salient point. To highlight an important message, use words such as "What's essential to remember is . . ." or "Here's the critical point. . . ."

Balance brevity with interesting detail. Ideally, your responses will be noteworthy and memorable. You will also want many of them to be brief so you can maintain the interactive nature of Q&A.

- *Make your responses interesting.* Vivid words and well-crafted sound bites are captivating; rambling explanations are not. An example or anecdote that didn't fit into your talk might resurface as part of an interesting response.

- *Use brief responses or well-structured longer ones.* If people's hands go up before you finish, either your comments aren't brief enough or you are not clearly wrapping them up. While brief replies hold people's interest, sometimes a question will require a detailed explanation. In such cases, begin with an overview that gives the audience an idea of how you plan to reply and end by using a strong, clear voice, followed by silence, to signal that you are done.

Keep everyone involved. Paraphrasing the hard-to-hear questions is one way to keep everyone aware of what's being discussed. In addition, call on people from various parts of the room, perhaps alternating from one section of the audience to another as you take questions. When speaking to those in the front, use enough volume so people in the back can hear. And don't just look at the questioner when you respond; focus on other audience members, too.

4. Listen for challenging questions.

Tough questions come in all shapes and sizes, but they tend to fall into three categories: (1) unclear questions, (2) questions framed in a limiting way, and (3) questions you can't answer.

Unclear questions: Perhaps you've used your best listening skills, but you still have no idea what you've been asked. When a question is unclear, use an "I" response rather than a "you" response. In other words, say "I'm not sure I understand the question" rather than "Your question is confusing." Sometimes the question is only a bit unclear. At such times, paraphrase to check that your assumptions are correct. In addition, be aware of three common types of unclear questions:

- *Vague questions* use nonspecific language. When you hear words such as "it," "this," "that notion," or "the other option," try to clarify your understanding of the vague words with a paraphrase.

- *Long multi-questions* string three, four, or even more questions together. Based on the situation and the questioner, you have several options in dealing with multi-questions: (1) synthesize all the questions and offer a single response, (2) start with the question you like best, avoiding the ones you don't want to address, and (3) answer one part of the question and ask the questioner to remind you of the remaining parts.

- *Broad questions* inquire about huge issues that could never be addressed in a limited time. To deal with them, either narrow the focus and respond to the question or point out the broad nature of the question and offer to address it later, perhaps after the presentation.

Limiting questions: Many types of questions seem to limit your options or lead you toward a response that you don't want to give. They include forced-choice, hypothetical, empty-chair, loaded-language, and false-premise questions. In addition, listen for distorted paraphrases that mischaracterize what you have said.

- *Forced-choice* questions imply there are a limited number of options and ask you to choose one. Often they use the word "or." For example, "What's more important, the amount of time a doctor can spend with each patient *or* the number of patients that can be seen each day?" Remember that "both" choices can be important. Other forced-choice structures ask you to rank items on the questioner's scale or to identify what's "most" significant. Once again, you can reframe the questions so you are setting the parameters.

- *Hypothetical* questions create a situation that doesn't exist, although it could be a potential reality. "If the FDA rejects your application, how will it affect other drugs in your research pipeline?" In such cases, it's best to stick with what is known rather than focus on what might occur. If the questioner is your boss, then you'll likely have to accept the premise; if the questioner is a reporter, then do not speculate.

- *Empty-chair* questions ask you to comment on something said by a third party, someone not in the room. If you didn't hear the CEO's comments or you haven't read the statement put out by the Attorney General, don't even begin to evaluate what was supposedly said or why it was said.

- *Loaded-language* questions include colorful words, phrases, and perhaps even sarcasm that make the question a minefield. Neutralize the language by using a paraphrase. Don't say, "I am not a heartless bureaucrat," instead say, "I know you're disappointed. I wish we had more resources so we could help everyone on the waiting list."

- *False-premise* questions begin with an incorrect assumption: "When did the accounting department begin falsifying their reports?" To respond, correct the assumption: "If you're concerned with the accuracy of our financial reports, let me assure you that we have open books and all our accounting practices are carefully monitored; we stand by our numbers."

- *Distorted paraphrases* aren't really questions; they are inaccurate summaries of your comments. For example, suppose you just finished explaining how your staffing levels would hold steady and someone distorts your remarks by saying: "So you're telling us layoffs are inevitable." Don't ignore these remarks. Correct them by saying, "Let me clarify: our staffing levels will be the same next year as they are this year."

"Don't know" questions: If you don't know the answer, don't bluff. Instead say, "I don't know." Or better, suggest where the person can find the answer. Or better yet, offer to get the answer yourself—"Off the top of my head, I don't know the demographics for that region, but I can easily get that information for you by tomorrow morning." Then be sure you follow up.

In other cases, you may just need a little time to gather your thoughts. If so, here are a few stalling options: (1) repeat or paraphrase the question, (2) turn the question outward by asking the questioner or the entire audience for their ideas and opinions, (3) take a moment to reflect by saying something such as "Fatima, let me think about your question for a second," or (4) write the question on a board or flipchart so you can discuss it as a group.

5. Control difficult or hostile audience members.

Occasionally, audience members don't have your best interest at heart. They may try to take control of the discussion, attack you or your ideas, or distract you in some way. If so, you need to control the situation without letting the confrontation get personal. Here are some techniques to handle hostility.

Types of difficult questioners and audience members: Different behaviors annoy different people, which means we can't possibly list all the ways audience members can be difficult. Nevertheless, here are a few of the troublesome types and how you might handle them:

- *Pontificators* enjoy the sound of their voices. They ramble on and on, sometimes never even asking a question. To respond, listen intently so you can paraphrase something of value and then bridge to a message that gets you back on track.

- *Nitpickers* focus on minutiae and take you off message. You can acknowledge that "yes, the actual figure is 14.89 percent" and then explain that you would like to focus on trends rather than on specific data points during your talk.

- *Needlers* use sarcasm or try to belittle you in some way. Don't mimic their sarcastic tone or try to embarrass them. Just restate your opinions calmly and clearly, using logical reasoning to back your views.

- *Distracters* initiate side conversations, roll their eyes, or mumble disapprovingly under their breath. You can move toward people having side conversations or pointedly wait until they stop talking, but don't become overly confrontational. Focus on the people who are interested instead.

General tips for handling a hostile audience member: How you manage the interaction between you and a hostile questioner will depend on many variables. For instance, you would deal differently with a hostile boss than you would a nasty colleague. Yet, in all cases, you want to maintain your credibility by being scrupulously polite, trying to find points of mutual agreement, using effective listening skills, and connecting with the audience members who are willing to be fair.

- *Be polite,* even to the rudest audience members. For example, don't snap at a pontificator by saying "So, what exactly is your point?" Of all the tips for handling difficult audiences, being polite is the most important.

- *Lessen hostility* by agreeing to disagree and pointing to common ground. For example, say something such as, "We don't seem to agree on how to handle this customer service problem, but since we agree that we want to do what's best for our customers, we can begin by conducting an assessment of their needs and views."

- *Paraphrase the feelings behind the question.* If the nonverbal behavior implies that there's more to the message than the words alone indicate, acknowledge the questioner's emotions in your paraphrase by noting the anger or frustration.

- *Stop repeat offenders tactfully,* perhaps by putting up your hand and explaining, "I'm sorry to interrupt, but I want to make sure we end on time, so let me touch on the issue you mentioned by saying. . . ."

- *Look elsewhere afterward.* After responding, do not direct your eye contact toward the difficult questioner. If you do, you're just inviting this person to make another challenging comment. Instead, look at the friendly faces so you can avoid repeated volleys with the troublemaker. Also be sure to look at supportive faces when you finish your talk; you don't want to invite another outburst during the closing moments of your talk.

6. Deal with online comments.

Audience members can also interact through what is called the "backchannel." It's what some audience members might be using to chat online during your presentation. These interactions usually take place via microblogs—such as Twitter—but they may take place through chat rooms, email, blogging, and so on.

Consider the pros and cons. On the plus side, tapping into the backchannel gives you another way to connect with your audience. It can engage some audience members and offer them an appealing way to ask questions and share feedback. It can also help a presenter broadcast messages to a wider audience. On the downside, online comments often create a distraction and interfere with listening. Since many people send out messages they would never say, it also increases the chances that people will share unflattering or even hostile comments.

Decide how to deal with the backchannel. Consider the audience's expectations, your role, and your preference.

- *Ignore the backchannel.* If you aren't comfortable with it and your audience isn't likely to use it, then you might not want to pay attention to the backchannel.

- *Curtail or control it.* If you have a client who demands confidentiality, you might choose to keep tablets, laptops, and phones out of the conference room. In other cases, you might not be able to ban the technology, but you might be able explain your preferences, perhaps by asking people to save texting for breaks. In large auditoriums, you'll have little luck controlling people's use of technology.
- *Accept and use it.* If your audience is likely to be online during your talk and you are comfortable with the technology, consider using it to your advantage.

Find out how to manage online interactions. In his book, *The Backchannel,* Cliff Atkinson discusses how to effectively use online exchanges. He acknowledges that you can use various channels for these interactions, but he goes into great detail about how to use Twitter.

- *Create a Twitter account and hashtag (#).* Publicize your intention to include online comments. Put the hashtag on your welcoming slide and promote it throughout the presentation.
- *Make your presentation Twitter-friendly.* Create a few Twitter-sized messages—140 characters or less—and encourage your audience to broadcast them. Plan for frequent Twitter breaks; prepare slides that display the hashtag and note how long you will break to share and review comments.
- *Arrange for a session moderator.* This person can follow people's comments and questions and alert you to the messages you need to see.
- *Explain the backchannel in your opening.* Encourage online dialogue. Explain how it works to those not connected. Agree on guidelines.
- *Deal with negative tweets.* Acknowledge the negative message and ask for a show of hands. Does the audience want you to address the concerns or carry on? If most people want you to carry on, then tweeters will see they're in the minority. If lots of people agree with the tweeters, you'll want to address the negative points.

If you used both strategic and topical information to craft your content, you should now have an effective opening, body, and closing for your presentation. You should also have a good idea about the questions the audience will ask. Now you're ready to design visual aids.

CHAPTER 5 OUTLINE

   I. START WITH YOUR TITLES.
- 1. Identify what the audience needs to see.
- 2. Create titles that clarify your message.

   II. DESIGN A BASIC TEMPLATE.
- 1. Establishing a color scheme
- 2. Making typography decisions
- 3. Choosing simple backgrounds and layouts

   III. THINK VISUALLY AS YOU DESIGN.
- 1. Data-driven charts explain the numbers.
- 2. Concept diagrams depict ideas.
- 3. Photographs add interest.
- 4. Animation clarifies complex slides.
- 5. Text charts list important details.

   IV. EDIT YOUR EFFORTS.
- 1. Verify that the structure is clear.
- 2. Enhance the visual effect.
- 3. Proof and proof again.

CHAPTER 5

Design Your Visuals

Most presentations use visuals, with the two most common options being projected slides and bound pages, known as "decks" or "pitchbooks." Often these visuals are created using PowerPoint. When using this software to design your slides and deck pages, we suggest that you (1) start with your titles to save time and focus your efforts; (2) design a basic template to give your visuals a unified, uncluttered look; (3) think visually to create slides and pages that interest the audience; and (4) edit your efforts to make sure they deliver messages that are clear and correct.

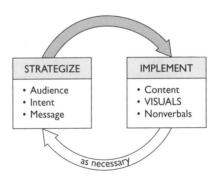

Slides and decks come in many varieties. Typically, slides are projected on a large screen and the presenter stands while using them. Decks tend to be used with smaller audiences and in a more interactive way. If you are deciding between a deck and a slide show, the table below summarizes their main differences.

COMPARING DECKS AND SLIDES		
	Decks	**Slides**
Presenter's position	Seated	Standing
In-depth discussion	More	Less
Words	More, using smaller fonts	Fewer, using larger fonts
Charts and diagrams	More complex; can be studied	Less complex; can be built
Advantages	+ Provide detailed hard copy + Allow people to skip ahead or return to a point + Can be read before or after the talk	+ Can direct all eyes to one point + Allow presenter to control flow of new information + Can be changed at last moment
Disadvantages	− Hard to keep everyone focused on the same point − Make establishing eye contact more difficult − Can become too detailed	− Less flexible, hard to skip points that are on the screen − Should not be used to show detailed material − May inhibit group discussion

In this chapter, we focus on printed decks and traditional slides. We also refer to a newer type of slide show, which uses what we call "image-driven" slides. These slide shows use more photographs and much less text than traditional ones.

- *To focus on slide design:* If you would like to learn more about how to simplify your slides, add eye-catching images, or use text creatively, look at Garr Reynolds' blog or his book *Presentation Zen Design*.

- *To explore template design:* For a look at how company templates can be effectively designed or to get some ideas you might want to try, look through Nancy Duarte's *slide:ology*.

- *To create bullet-free slides:* If you want to try a new way of using visuals, one without bullet lists, you may want to read Cliff Atkinson's *Beyond Bullet Points*.

I. START WITH YOUR TITLES.

You have already decided what to say. Now you need to determine what the audience needs to see. This section encourages you to list your titles before you begin making your slides or pages. It also introduces an important tool in your design kit—message titles.

1. Identify what the audience needs to see.

In our experience, we find that more presenters make too many visuals than too few. And even worse, they often try to cram too much on the ones they do make.

The number of slides or deck pages you will use depends on the situation. However, no matter what the situation, design only those slides and deck pages that (1) reinforce the structure of your talk, (2) emphasize your main messages, (3) draw attention to supporting points, or (4) help you respond to important questions. Also search for times *not* to use visuals—moments to keep the audience's attention focused solely on you.

Reinforcing the structure: One good reason to use slides or deck pages is to help the audience understand the structure of your talk.

- *Title slide or deck cover:* This visual highlights your name and the title of your talk. It should also introduce the color scheme and graphics used on later visuals.

- *Preview visual:* One of the most important slides or pages in your presentation is the preview visual. It may be an "agenda slide" that highlights the sections of your talk or your deck's "table of contents" page. Because it is so important, make your preview visual stand out.

- *Section visuals:* To clarify the structure of long presentations, you might also want section visuals, which are slides or deck pages that mark the beginning of a section. In a deck, you would use one of these visuals for each section listed in the table of contents. In a slide show, you might insert a copy of the preview slide at the start of each section. (For more information about how to use a preview slide as a section visual, see page 113.) With image-driven slides, you might choose to have distinct section visuals, with each section linked to one of your main points.

- *Executive summary deck page:* Some companies require a deck to include an executive summary. This page highlights conclusions or recommendations and explains the scope and flow of the deck. Don't use such text-heavy summaries in a slide show; find other ways to emphasize your conclusions or recommendations.

- *Closing visuals:* As explained on page 68, you may have two closing messages if you plan to take questions after your talk. You may decide to use a visual for one, both, or neither of these moments. A closing visual could focus on synthesizing your recommendations or highlighting a message that captures the essence of your presentation. In a slide show, it could be visual reminder of your main points or it could be nothing—just a black slide that allows you to move in front of the screen. Ask yourself exactly what you want to communicate during the final moments. That message should influence what you want the audience to see at the end of your talk.

Emphasizing main messages: For many presenters, limiting important messages is much more difficult than listing them. However, if you are having trouble generating a list of titles to turn into visual aids, try one or more of the following:

- *Look at your presentation objective for clues* about what needs to be seen as well as heard. For instance, if your objective identifies a sound bite you want the audience to remember, then you might want to use those words as a title on a visual aid. If you haven't done so already, you would also need to decide where this sound bite fits within the structure of your presentation.

- *Recall the focusing techniques* described on page 59. If you used something like the email technique, then you may find important messages embedded in that summary. If so, think about how those messages fit with the other titles you want to turn into visual aids.

- *Try making a storyboard,* as discussed on page 60. If you've already used this ordering technique, then you have sketches that represent possible visual aids. If you haven't done so already, create a headline for every storyboard box. Do those headlines make essential points? If so, add them to your list of titles; you will want to use them, along with the storyboard sketches, as a starting place for various slides or deck pages.

- *Focus on each section* or chunk individually. Sometimes identifying the main messages is easier if you break the job into smaller parts. Work first on whichever section seems easiest and then tackle the more challenging parts.

Drawing attention to supporting points: Some of your main messages might need extra visual emphasis. If so, think about the secondary points that support them. Backup visuals can be based on messages about quantitative data, examples, essential details, or benefit statements that explain what's in it for them. Resist creating a blizzard of backup points. Instead, be selective. Decide which points will (1) provide the strongest support and (2) make the most powerful visuals.

Preparing for Q&A: Maybe you think the audience will have a question you can address, but would rather not unless they bring it up. If so, think of a succinct message that supports your response and turn that message into a Q&A visual. In a slide show, these visuals are typically placed after the closing slide; in a deck, they appear in an appendix. The audience's interest will determine whether you use them.

Making yourself the visual: Sometimes the best visual is no visual. When you are giving a presentation, you may spontaneously decide to break away from your visuals to connect with your audience. Such moments can also be planned. For example, you can insert a black slide in your slide show or create a speaking note that reminds you to put aside the deck. Consider taking a visual aid break for one of these reasons:

- *To fix the flow:* Ideally, your list of titles will have a logical flow. If it doesn't, you can change a message, cut one, add one, rearrange the list, or plan to fix the flow yourself by taking attention away from the visuals, connecting with the audience for a reason, and then segueing back to the visuals.

- *To add emphasis to an important section:* Section visuals provide a good place to stop and take a real break, but they are also an easy place to take a visual aid break. For example, you might set the deck aside and tell a story that sums up the importance of the previous section or start a new section by explaining why you are passionate about what's coming next.

- *To give the audience a change of pace:* Critique your list. Imagine what sort of image will result from each title: is the message most likely to become a chart, diagram, photo, or list? If you spot a sequence that has too many lists or one that bombards the audience with charts and numbers, you might want to cut a title or plan a visual aid break, a place where you will communicate directly to your audience, without support from a visual aid.

2. Create titles that clarify your message.

Some slides and deck pages use "topic titles," such as "Marketing Strategy" or "Survey Results." These titles tell people what is being discussed, but they don't tell them what to see. On the other hand, more effective "message titles" specify your point and speed up information sharing. Having a message title also enables a visual to make sense on its own. Most importantly, it indicates how to design a slide or page.

Specify your point. Look at the following column charts. The first one uses a topic title: "Home Sales by Quarter." It lets the audience decide what point the image is making. The second chart shows the same data, but this version uses a message title. It tells the audience exactly what to see. The chart could have had many other message titles, such as (1) "Home Sales Are Increasing," (2) "Sales More Than Doubled in the Second Quarter," or (3) "First Quarter Sales Were Exceptionally Low." Notice that all these message titles include a verb. Sometimes just adding a verb and a little detail will make your point clear.

Example: ineffective topic title   *Example: effective message title*

   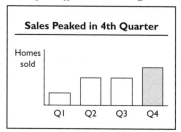

Speed up information sharing. Titles are large, often boldface, and should be placed where the audience looks first—at the top of the slide or page. If they contain a message, then that message will influence what viewers see as their eyes move around the rest of the screen or page. Once your audience sees your main point, they have an easier time taking in the details.

Message titles tend to be longer than topical ones; however, don't make them too complex or they will fail to do their job. For example, if everyone is reading a 12-word title, then no one will be listening to you. Therefore, strive for brevity—the briefer the better, as long as the title communicates your point. The following table shows how a vague topic title can be switched to a more descriptive one.

FROM TOPIC TO MESSAGE TITLE	
Vague topic title . . .	**. . . transformed into a clearer message title**
Agenda: Bard Real Estate	Build Bard's Community Connections
Recommendations	Follow Four Steps to a Four-Star Rating
Summer Web Traffic	Web Traffic Soared in June
Budget Allocation	Salaries Were 30% of the Budget
Survey Results	The Economy Was the #1 Concern
Experience vs. Sales	Experienced Brokers Sold More Bonds

Create stand-alone sense. Sometimes your visuals need to make sense when you aren't there to explain them. Message titles are the first step in creating that stand-alone sense, something that can aid both the audience and the presenter.

- *Prepare the audience:* When decks make stand-alone sense, people can use them to prepare for a discussion.
- *Help viewers follow along:* Message titles help distracted listeners reconnect with the current point. They are especially helpful during online presentations.
- *Provide useful records:* PowerPoint files that make sense on their own are often more useful than those that don't. For example, one way to make people more aware of your talk is to upload your slides online. However, unless the images make stand-alone sense, they'll be of little value to those who download them.

Influence design decisions: The PowerPoint defaults are set up for extremely large titles. We explain how to make adjustments for message titles in the next section. However, other design choices should also be based on your message titles.

- *Create images that match your message.* Your title helps you decide whether a chart, diagram, drawing, map, or photograph will best communicate your point. For example, on pages 100–102 we show how pinpointing your message enables you to discover what type of chart to use. Similarly, on page 105, we explain the importance of matching the visual message of a diagram to the verbal message in your title.

- *Make highlighting decisions based on the title.* How you use color and graphics should be based on your title. We explain how to choose "spot" and "dimming" colors on page 89 and include some suggestions about how to use arrows or other graphics as highlighting tools on page 114.

Adapt to the situation. Your message title should drive the design of the visual. However, after you have used it to create your image, in some cases, you may want to edit or even delete it.

- *When words are implied:* Sometimes you can cut part of a title, perhaps even the verb, and the message will still be clear. For instance, "Four Steps to Four Stars" grabs more attention than "Follow Four Steps to a Four-Star Rating," and it will still guide your design efforts better than "Recommendations."

- *When a less direct message is the better option:* Suppose your boss expects to see the latest sales figures in your deck, so you designed a chart that shows the steep decline featured in your message title. However, if you don't want to be the harbinger of bad news, then do what media trainers have termed "blanding it out." Don't emphasize a message you don't want to deliver. Instead, include the required chart, but use a nondescript title. Similarly, if "Build Bard's Community Connections" sounds a little too direct, then simply change "Build" to "Building." The change will soften the tone, but still let viewers know the focus of your visual.

- *When a slide image works by itself:* Suppose one of the messages you listed is captured by a photograph. In such cases, a title might not be necessary since you found a picture that communicates your point. In other cases, adding a word or phrase on top of the image might be enough to clarify your meaning. If a photo works without a message title, then let it fill up the screen.

II. DESIGN A BASIC TEMPLATE.

Before you insert your titles into a PowerPoint presentation, find what's called the "Master View." Once you are in this view, you can use the "Slide Master" to design slides or pages that look unified.

Why create your own master when dozens of prepared ones are available? The main reason is that many prepared templates have distracting elements that interfere with your titles, text, diagrams, and charts. Although you can alter them to make them usable, it's just as easy to design your own. In this section, we'll explain how, by discussing color schemes, typography, backgrounds, and layouts for your slide show or deck.

I. Establishing a color scheme

Rather than using the overly colorful PowerPoint options, we suggest creating your own color scheme. To do so, (1) consider the audience, (2) choose a background color, (3) select visible title and text colors, (4) pick a "spot color," (5) include dimming options, and (6) make sure the colors work together.

Consider the audience. Before you settle on any color, think about your audience. People do not view or interpret color the same way. Some of their reactions might be based on cultural associations, while others might be more specific to individuals.

- *National, religious, and other cultural differences:* When you are presenting in a new culture, ask how colors are viewed. For example, many people have strong associations with the colors in their country's flag. Colors may also have ceremonial connotations; weddings, for example, are linked with white, yellow, or red in various cultures.

- *Business considerations:* Like nations, many organizations have colors, with blue a traditional favorite in terms of corporate logos and green a common choice for ecologically focused enterprises. Choose colors appropriate for your industry and company. If you are new to an organization, be careful not to use a competitor's colors as your color scheme.

- *Color blindness:* Even if your corporate colors are red and green, they might not be the right ones to use. About 5%–10% of the population sees both colors as gray.

Choose a background color. The background color depends on the type of visual—whether you are projecting images, printing a deck, or coordinating a slide show with a handout. It will be influenced by projection and printing equipment, logo colors, visibility issues, audience expectations, and your preferences.

- *Projected slides:* You can use a dark background—for instance, black or dark blue. Choosing black will cause the background to blend with the screen, but make the objects on your slide look vibrant. Choosing blue will be a safe option, since it is often used for corporate presentations. For a less formal look, pick a light color. A white background may add so much brightness to a room that you won't be tempted to dim any lights. However, in some rooms white can pose a problem: if the screen is large and the slides sparsely designed, then a white background can cause an annoying glare. Avoid colors that are not dark or light; they won't provide enough contrast for your text choices.

- *Decks:* White is a great background choice for printed pages. Light colors, such as cream, beige, or pale blue, are also options. Bright and dark backgrounds are less desirable; they use lots of toner, so they are more expensive to produce and can look streaky or faded when the printer's toner runs low.

- *Black and white printouts:* White is the best background choice for handouts. If you plan to use two-sided printing to save paper, then also avoid using large black or dark gray shapes because they will be visible on the back side of standard-weight paper.

Some visuals use two background colors. Some slide shows, particularly image-driven ones, use more than one background color. Although this choice makes creating a color scheme more complex, the different backgrounds can be used to show hierarchy, as shown below.

Background 1 Main Layout	Background 1 Second Layout	Background 2 Third Layout
For the opening (including preview)	For each new section (the main points)	For backup points

Select title and text colors. You can't read yellow print on a white page or see black numbers on a dark blue screen. You need far more contrast to make your words and numbers stand out. With dark blue slides, all the options listed in the following table would work for titles, but some might not be good for other text. (For example, white is a safe choice for regular text on a dark slide; however, bright yellow text could make the details look more prominent than the title.) For white deck pages, choose black for regular text and save the other options for titles or labels.

CONTRASTING COLOR COMBINATIONS	
For a background that is a . . .	**. . . try one of these title or text colors for contrast**
Dark blue slide	White, peach, yellow, gold, pink, lavender, light blue, light green, aqua, beige, or light sage green. Pale colors will look white.
White deck page	Black, bold colors (blue, red, orange, green, or purple), or dark colors (navy blue, hunter green, brown, maroon, rust, indigo, slate, or teal).

Pick a "spot color." In addition to your background, title, and text colors, choose a spot color—an accent color that will work like a spotlight, focusing attention on your most important ideas. Make the spot color the boldest of your palette. Use it sparingly for items that need attention, such as the center of your diagram. (If you are editing a PowerPoint color scheme, avoid inserting this color as the "Fill" or "Accent Color 1"; otherwise, it will pop up every time you insert a line or shape.)

Add dimming options. Colors used to dim items do the opposite of spot color: they communicate "look somewhere else." Gray is a safe dimming choice, but other colors mixed with gray may also work. For example, if your spot color is bright blue, then a pale gray-blue might work well for less important items. In a slide show, you may want to dim text on a list. Again, gray is a good choice, but you can also use a variation of your background color. For example, on a purple background, a slightly lighter purple could do the job.

Make sure the colors work together. The color scheme needs to use a limited number of colors that all look good together. To find them, use PowerPoint's "Custom Color Screen," which is shown below.

❶ *The custom color box:* You will find bold, pure colors at the top and more subdued ones lower in the box.

❷ *The white- to- black bar:* Modify the lightness or darkness of your selections with the vertical bar to the right, which adds varying amounts of white or black.

❸ *The sample box:* This box shows the color you have found.

❹ *The RGB values:* Whenever you locate a color you like, write down the numbers in the boxes labeled "Red," "Green," and "Blue," so you can create the color again by using those numbers.

If you need more detailed instructions for using PowerPoint, see *Guide to PowerPoint*, listed on page 145 in the Bibliography.

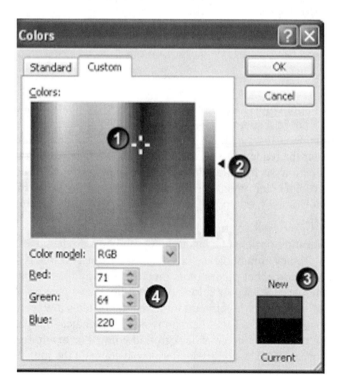

In general, limit your palette to three colors in addition to black, gray, and white. If you opt to use more, avoid what graphic artist Jan White calls "the fruit salad effect"—a kaleidoscope of colors that may look festive, but doesn't make anything stand out.

- *Limit yourself to one dramatic color.* If all the colors are exceptionally vibrant—such as fire-engine red, neon green, and flamingo pink—they will compete with each other and possibly create a juvenile look more suitable for a children's classroom than a company's conference room. Using more than one bold color also makes your job harder; it will be much easier to emphasize your message if other colors don't compete with your spot color.

- *Experiment with less intense colors.* Using PowerPoint's Custom Color Screen, you can transform exceptionally bold colors into more subdued ones. To make colors less dominant, mix them with some gray, black, or white. For example, to make fire-engine red less eye-catching, add some black and you will end up with maroon. To tone down neon green, move your curser down the Custom Color Screen box until you find sage, a mixture of green and gray, which looks more subtle. To soften flamingo pink, just add white.

- *Try complementary colors.* Bold opposites (such as purple and yellow or blue and orange) can be attractive pairings if you make some adjustments. For instance, combine a dark purple background with gold titles and white text or use a navy blue background with peach titles and white text. These combinations offer a high degree of contrast and provide visual interest.

- *Test deck colors on hard copy.* Prepare a color sample page, using several variations of the colors you have selected. Identify them by the numbers that appear on the Custom Color Screen. Print the page so you can see which variations look the best. If your deck has a colored background, test how each color looks on the background. Save the test page; it may be a useful way to compare colors if your deck is photocopied or produced with a different printer.

- *Test slide colors on the big screen.* If possible, check your colors with the equipment you will be using. If such a test isn't possible, plan to make last-minute adjustments. The colors on your computer will look different than those on the big screen. The biggest difference will be that many colors will seem washed out, so be sure to check them all, paying special attention to light or pale colors, which may just look white. Some colors may even change hues. For example, sometimes yellow looks green on the screen, while peach appears yellow.

2. Making typography decisions

PowerPoint offers more than 100 fonts, but please don't feel obliged to use them all. Some are serif fonts, which have little strokes at the ends of the letters. Others are sans serif fonts, which don't have these flourishes. Many of the fancy options were designed for posters or party invitations.

You want to choose a very legible font for your visual aids—one that makes it simple to decipher the individual letters. Once you've picked a legible font, you want to use it in a way that makes it easy to read all the words and numbers on your slides or deck pages.

Limit yourself to one or two fonts. The best way to ensure that your title and text fonts work together is to use the same choice for both. However, many decks use two fonts, one for titles and the other for text. When using two fonts, make sure your choices contrast and complement each other. The easiest way to make them contrast is to choose one serif and one sans serif option. The only way to see whether they complement one another is to experiment; see how they look on a deck page.

- *Serif fonts:* In general, serif fonts create a classic impression. The little flourishes on these fonts tend to make individual letters easy to identify. This enhanced legibility is noticeable on a printed page (rather than on a screen) because printing produces sharp images. However, some serif fonts aren't the best option for text viewed on a screen. Always test those that use thin lines to form all or part of the letters; sometimes the thin strokes are hard to see when the font is projected.

  Examples of serif fonts, for a more classic look
  Cambria, Times New Roman, Georgia

- *Sans serif fonts:* "Sans" means "without," so these fonts don't have the little flourishes. Their streamlined letter forms make them appear more modern or high tech. A standard sans serif font, like the following examples, can be a great choice for projection, a very good choice for deck titles, and a readable choice for blocks of text in a deck page or handout.

  Examples of sans serif fonts, for a more modern look
  Calibri, Arial, Gill Sans MT

Consider the variation among fonts. In addition to the serif and sans serif distinction, fonts vary in other ways. To do a better job selecting them, learn how to spot several differences.

- *Compare the height of "Example" letters.* Fonts use their height (also known as "point size") in different ways. Some devote much of their height to regular, lower case letters like an "x," while others devote a lot of this vertical space to letter parts that extend up or down, like the low tail on a "p." If you test a font by typing the word "Example," you can compare the height of its "x" to the height of its "p" and "l." The relative size of the "x" is what designers call "x-height." It has a big impact on how large your font looks. (Verdana text looks bigger than Perpetua because it has a larger x-height.)

  Examples: both 12-point fonts, but different x-heights

  # Verdana Example
  Perpetua Example

- *Notice letter width and spacing.* Some fonts are wide and rounded, with lots of space between letters. Many of these fonts are easy to read, but they can be challenging to use if you have long message titles or complex labels. Narrow fonts fit into small spaces; however, make sure their condensed spacing doesn't make them hard to read.

  Examples: different widths and spacing

  Bookman Old Style
  Arial Narrow

- *Expand your options by using "families."* A family includes a basic font and several variations. For example, if you check PowerPoint's font options, you will find Arial, Arial Black, and Arial Narrow. They could be used together because they are part of the same family, with Arial Black having an extremely heavy, extended appearance, which might make it useful if you were putting one big word on a photograph, and Arial Narrow using slim, tightly spaced letters, which might enable it to fit into small spaces.

- *Create the right impression.* Arial is one of the most common sans serif choices; Times New Roman is a top choice among serif fonts. Both are very legible. However, if you wanted a fresh, atypical look, then neither of these options would create that impression.

Make lettering large enough to be seen. Fonts are sized in points, with a 72-point font being an inch, a 36-point font being half an inch, and so on. PowerPoint allows you to choose from a list of point sizes, but you can also customize any size you want; for instance, you can change the "20" in the box that shows font size to "21" and hit the "Enter" key to make text just a bit larger.

Because of the variation among fonts, providing size guidelines for the words and numbers on your visuals is difficult. Nevertheless, we will suggest some possibilities. If a font has a small x-height, start at the higher end of the range; if it has a large x-height, try the smaller options first.

- *For projection:* The distance between the projector and the screen will greatly affect the size of your words and numbers. If you can't test your font sizes with the projector and screen you will be using, then start with these parameters: (1) make your titles larger than other text, but small enough to work with your longest message title, somewhere between 28 and 40 point; (2) make the text used in bullet lists clearly smaller than the title, but large enough to be seen—perhaps 20 to 30 point for the main text and smaller for secondary text such as diagram labels; (3) be sure the text for chart numbers or sources is visible—perhaps 14 to 18 point.

- *For decks:* Use font sizes that are large enough for audience members to glance down and easily read the deck when it is placed on a table. You might try 18- to 24-point titles and 14- to 18-point text. Be careful with the small lettering used for labels or sources; older eyes may have trouble seeing tiny 8-, 9-, and even some 10-point fonts. If a deck is to be used more like a handout or distributed before your talk, then you can include more detail and smaller fonts since audience members won't be reading as you speak. In these cases, you might try 14- or 16-point titles and 11- or 12-point text.

- *For handouts based on your slides:* If your slides are simply designed, then the words on your handouts should be visible if you print two slide images per page. However, realize that 16-point text on your slide will only be 8 point in this format.

Enhance readability. PowerPoint tempts you with many ways to alter and format text. These choices will influence the readability of your slides and deck pages and you should make them while you are designing the Slide Master.

- *Choose simple style options.* Wise choices for titles include plain text or bold. Avoid mixing several styles together (for example, a bold, italicized, shadow effect), which results in "letter junk." On the Slide Master, make the title bold if there isn't a clear variation between your title and text size. Do not, however, make the bullet text bold because that will make your slides and deck pages look too heavy and fail to make anything stand out.

- *Avoid all capital letters.* GRAPHIC DESIGN PROFESSOR LISA GRAHAM OFFERS THIS DOCUMENT DESIGN ADVICE: "AVOID ALL CAPS LIKE THE PLAGUE." LONG LINES OF CAPITALIZED TEXT ARE HARD TO READ AND CAN BE INTERPRETTED AS "SHOUTING" AT YOUR AUDIENCE, SO DON'T USE ALL CAPS AS PART OF YOUR MASTER.

- *Select an alignment for your titles.* Left justification is frequently a good choice for your titles. However, if all your message titles are short, you might decide to center them. Centering creates a more formal impression, but it looks much better with charts and diagrams than it does with bullet lists. In addition, if titles wrap to a second line, centering them often looks odd; left justification tends to looks better and it enhances readability.

- *Test the "Line Spacing."* If you plan to use text that will wrap to a second line, then test the spacing. If text lines look too close together, go to "Line Spacing Options" and select the exact spacing you want. Base your choice on the font's point size and its x-height. For small to medium text fonts with an average x-height, try making the spacing 2- to 4-points larger than the text. If you have selected a medium font with a large x-height (for example, Verdana), then you will need to increase the line spacing even more.

- *Check the "Paragraph Spacing."* Although you won't be writing paragraphs, also adjust what's called the "Paragraph Spacing." It's the space that is inserted when you hit the "Enter" key, such as the space between bulleted items on a list. You want the space that separates two bullets to look larger than the space between two lines of text within a bullet.

- *Use simple, filled bullets.* Choose simple, filled bullets (such as • or ◆) making sure they are large enough to be seen, but not overpowering. Avoid fancy options (such as ➢ or ◼), which draw too much attention to themselves. When choosing a color for your bullet character, either match the text color or choose a subtle one. If you need second-level bullets, use a dash or small dot. Delete third-, fourth-, and fifth-level bullets, so you won't be tempted to use them.

3. Choosing simple backgrounds and layouts

Creating visuals with a unified, simple look requires some planning and lots of restraint. Whatever flourishes you add to the background will make your job more complex.

When you design the Slide Master, you will be using various PowerPoint tools to help you position words and images in a consistent way. These tools work fairly well for slides, but they were not intended for decks; therefore, we suggest a few ways to deal with deck design issues.

Choosing a solid background: A solid background is the safest choice. Adding color variations may make a background look more interesting, but it will also affect the visibility of some text and require you to understand how to work with light and shadows. The worst mistakes involve adding detailed images across a large portion of the background. Such designs limit the space you can use and add a needless distraction.

Designer Nancy Duarte suggests that you think of your background like a canvas—a surface to hold all the content you will place on it. She thinks that canvas should be simple. If you opt to alter it, do so for a reason:

- *Inserting a line to emphasize a title:* To separate the title from the other text, you can draw a line under it. This addition helps if your title and text are the same color or a little too similar in size. When you select a line color, choose something visible, yet subtle.

- *Inserting a band of color:* Page 88 shows two ways to use bands of color. You might decide to use a narrow band across the bottom or a wide one in the middle.

- *Including a logo:* Make sure your background looks good with the logo or find out if it is acceptable to use either a "reverse image" (for example, a logo shown in all white rather than black) or a "grayscale" version of the logo, which is a color image transformed to black, grays, and white. Avoid plopping a logo with a white background on a colored slide; ask for a transparent background instead. Some logos take up lots of room, so think before you decide to include them on your master. You may want to use a logo only on some slides or pages.

Modifying placeholders: Placeholders confine text or images within a specific area. If you add background designs, you may need to move the title and text placeholders to accommodate the changes.

The following image shows the various placeholders on the master: ❶ a title placeholder, ❷ a text placeholder, ❸ a date placeholder, ❹ a footer placeholder, and ❺ a page number placeholder. When you make changes to a placeholder on the master, those changes affect the corresponding placeholders on your other slides or pages. You probably won't use all these placeholders as you design. For example, you need page numbers on a deck, but you may not want them on your slides.

Positioning design elements on the Slide Master: PowerPoint also includes tools to help you position placeholders and graphics. The "Rulers" appear above and to the side of the slide; they help you locate the slide's center and gauge the space between objects. The "Grid" is meant to be a crude approximation of a tool used by professional designers. These dotted lines make it easier to align and place objects on slides.

The "Slide Layouts" arrange the placeholders in various ways; some allow text or charts to extend across most of the screen, while others divide this space in half. If you make changes to placeholders, make sure they are used consistently on all the master layouts.

Modifying the "Slide Master" for a deck: Decks are prone to more design errors than slides. Since deck pages hold more content than slides, many presenters put far too much on them. In addition, the prepared layouts were created for slides with large fonts; smaller fonts are very hard to read when they are formatted the same way. Therefore, it takes more work to design a good master for a deck page.

- *Remember the invisible margin.* When you print your deck, a half-inch margin, not visible on the screen, will be added around the page.

- *Consider adjusting the margins.* Using larger margins may improve the look of your deck, especially since part of the top margin may be used for the spiral binding; however, don't just add space to the top. The bottom margin should be noticeably larger than the top one to prevent text and images from looking as if they are sliding down the page.

- *Modify the Slide Master.* The simplest way to adjust the Slide Master is to decrease the width of title and text placeholders so they don't extend across more than two-thirds to three-fourths of the deck page. If a text placeholder allows you to create lines that use more than 10 words per line, then it is probably too wide for the font size. Either decrease the width of the placeholders, or increase the size of the text, or use column layouts for your text. Keep charts and diagrams the same width as your text placeholder. Create a sample page and check "Print Preview" to see if you need to adjust the master.

Designing a title master: Although the title slide or deck cover will use a different layout than the other slides or pages, this image needs to coordinate with those that follow. Ideally, you want to feature your spot color somewhere on this slide or page. Also think about the content you need to put on the title visual and arrange the layout so you can group items that belong together.

Using a company template: Company templates can save you time; however, some are challenging to use. Here are two possible quick fixes:

- *Background distractions:* If the master features a busy background design, create a layout that uses a solid background color. Use it for slides featuring charts or diagrams.

- *Overly prominent logo:* Ask if you can omit the logo on slides that use charts, diagrams, and photos and feature it on title and text slides. With a deck, see if the logo can be shown in grayscale so it won't interfere with the spot color on your charts and diagrams.

TIPS FOR DESIGNING A TEMPLATE

Getting started	Find the Master View. Use a plain, simple background and skip prepared PowerPoint templates and design themes.
Choosing colors	Use the "Custom Color Screen" to choose colors that 1. are appropriate for the audience, 2. provide contrast between the background and content, 3. include a spot color and dimming options.
Limiting colors	Avoid the "fruit salad effect" by limiting your scheme to three colors plus black, white, and gray. Use only one bold color as the spot color.
Selecting fonts	Choose one or two legible fonts: 1. one font in various sizes for titles, text, labels, and so on; 2. one font plus a variation from the same "family"; 3. two complementary fonts.
Sizing fonts	In addition to point size, remember that x-height and the thickness and shape of letters influence how large the font will look. Use the following ranges to test visibility. *For slides:* Titles from 28- to 40-point Main text from 20- to 30-point *For decks:* Titles about 18- to 24-point Main text about 14- to 18-point
Formatting titles and text	Use simple styles. Bold is good for titles, but don't use it on all text. Avoid PowerPoint temptations known as "letterjunk."
Customizing the line spacing	Test spacing between text lines. Use the "Paragraph Spacing" screen to increase line spacing; add even more space between the bullet points.
Adding graphics to the master	Add graphics for a reason. Use the rulers and the grid lines to position them.
Modifying placeholders	Delete placeholders you don't need. When altering a placeholder, check the effect on others.

III. THINK VISUALLY AS YOU DESIGN.

Once you have a well-designed template, focus on the content you will put on each slide or page. Use charts, diagrams, photographs, and other options, so your visual aids are actually visual.

1. Data-driven charts explain the numbers.

Every table of numbers offers scores of potential messages. It's your job to locate these messages, decide which ones are relevant, and turn the corresponding numbers into accurate and easy-to-comprehend charts. To do so, follow Gene Zelazny's method: (1) determine your message; (2) identify the comparison; and (3) select the chart form. Using this approach, we'll examine four data comparisons.

Time series (changes over time): With this comparison, time is plotted on the x-axis. The change can be measured in seconds, days, or even decades; the message can focus on increases, steady growth, or an unexpected decline. If your message is about a pattern occurring over time, then you have three options: column, line, or area charts.

- *Choose column charts for limited data points* and for times when you want to emphasize specific numbers as much as the trend. To make your column chart more visual, increase the width of the columns and reduce the space between them. Delete details that distract from your message, as explained on page 116.

- *Use line charts to emphasize trends.* When you have many data points, a line chart will show the trend more elegantly than columns. Unfortunately, PowerPoint doesn't make very effective line charts. To improve their look, set the trend line to at least a 4-point width and use a visible color. Save dotted lines for times when you are forecasting trends. Always eliminate the "chartjunk" as shown on page 115. And don't use more than three trend lines, or you may end up with a tangled mess, which Zelazny has dubbed "a spaghetti chart."

- *Be careful with area charts.* Because an area chart colors the space under the trend line, this chart looks more dramatic than a line chart. However, don't use area charts to show more than a single trend or the resulting stacks will confuse viewers.

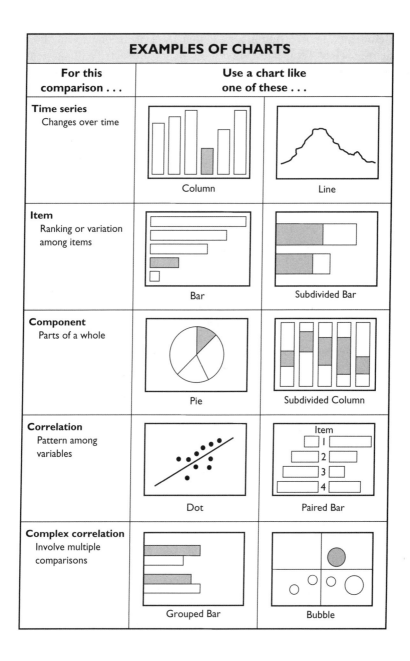

EXAMPLES OF CHARTS

For this comparison . . .	Use a chart like one of these . . .	
Time series Changes over time	Column	Line
Item Ranking or variation among items	Bar	Subdivided Bar
Component Parts of a whole	Pie	Subdivided Column
Correlation Pattern among variables	Dot	Paired Bar
Complex correlation Involve multiple comparisons	Grouped Bar	Bubble

Item (ranking or variation among items): An item comparison ranks items, such as companies, survey results, or products. With an item comparison, the message isn't about time. It's about how certain items are similar or which one ranks first, third, or even last. For such comparisons, use a simple bar chart. Bar charts are easy to label because you can insert the label beside or even on the bar.

Component (parts of a whole): A component comparison shows the relationship among parts of a whole. Your message might be about percentages, shares, or proportions. For components of one item, choose a pie chart; for components of multiple items, you will probably select another option.

- *Choose pie charts for simple comparisons.* Pie charts are easy to make, which may explain why they are sometimes overused. If you are projecting a pie chart, limit the number of slices; more than six will be difficult to differentiate and label. If you are featuring one slice, put it at the "12 o'clock" position of the pie. In all cases, eliminate the legend and label your pie slices as we did on page 115.

- *Consider other choices for multiple component comparisons.* If the message is about how one budget component changes over time, then use subdivided columns, with a y-axis that goes from 0% to 100%. message isn't linked to time, then consider subdivided bars, with an x-axis that goes from 0% to 100%.

Correlation (pattern between variables): These comparisons show the relationship—or lack of relationship—between two variables. For example, perhaps you want to show that the most expensive canned foods received the highest taste-test ratings. To show the pattern between price and ratings, you could choose a dot chart or paired bars, depending on how many food items were in the data pool.

- *Try dot charts when you have many data points.* If you were plotting the price and ratings for 20 items, then your best option would be to plot each point with a dot and insert a line to show the pattern.

- *Use paired bars for limited data points.* If comparing the price and ratings for four items, then use paired bars, as shown on page 101.

- *Be careful with complex correlation comparisons.* Be especially careful with bubble charts, which are dot charts with an extra dimension: the size of the dot. These charts need to be built gradually and explained carefully.

2. Concept diagrams depict ideas.

While data-driven charts help people understand your quantitative messages, concept diagrams enable them to picture your qualitative ideas. Lines, shapes, and your imagination are the building blocks of diagrams. You can easily find examples that illustrate relationships or indicate sequences. With a little more effort, you can also find ways to communicate less common ideas.

Some diagrams illustrate relationships. On the following page, you will find examples of diagrams that show how items or ideas interact, how they are structured, and how they compare.

- *To show interaction:* You can use overlapping circles (known as a Venn diagram) to show the intersection of two or more ideas. Or, you can show that ideas are connected by placing them along a shape's perimeter and inserted dotted lines or arrows, as we did with the AIM triangle on page 2. You can also combine arrows and shapes to depict how some items are influencing others.

- *To emphasize structure:* Organizational charts and idea charts show how people, positions, or ideas are linked. A pyramid diagram, which is shown on page 104, emphasizes the foundation of a structure. If items are organized around a hub or core idea, then a honeycomb pattern, or something similar, can communicate that point.

- *To compare concepts:* A T-chart can be used to separate items so they can be viewed side by side. For more complex interactions, consider a matrix, which divides space into quadrants.

Other diagrams highlight sequence. They can show the steps in a process, the order of events, or the repetition of stages.

- *To indicate linear flow:* Arrows, chevrons, and lines can show movement. A chevron is a good way to highlight the stages of a project. A series of shapes linked by a line or arrows will also communicate linear flow.

- *To show time sequence:* Time lines can illustrate events over time. Gantt charts are a type of time line; they position bars over a time line to show the starting and stopping points for stages of a project.

- *To depict circular flow:* When flow isn't linear, use curved arrows to show how stages repeat. Linking shapes with curved arrows or a circle can also depict this flow.

EXAMPLES OF DIAGRAMS

To show . . .	. . . use a diagram like one of these:	
Interaction	Venn Diagram	Arrow and Shapes
Structure	Pyramid Diagram	Honeycomb Diagram
Comparison	T-Chart	Matrix
Linear flow	Chevron	Gantt Chart
Circular flow	Cycle	Stages in a Cycle

Uncommon diagrams stand out. A chevron is common. Its familiarity makes its meaning easy to grasp. However, common diagrams also have drawbacks: they aren't as interesting as a novel approach and they may not work for your message. For instance, you need an atypical diagram, perhaps something similar to the one below, to show that a big change is pulling others behind it.

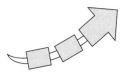

Find inspiration from many sources. For people who have trouble visualizing concepts as diagrams, PowerPoint added a feature called "SmartArt." Because we are willing to bet that you are smarter than this art, we recommend you look for diagram ideas outside PowerPoint. Books such as *Say It with Charts* and *Blah, Blah, Blah* offer dozens of ideas. If you look at them and start to doodle, you will come up with new possibilities. If, however, you do use SmartArt, you can "Ungroup" a prepared diagram to delete parts you don't want; you can even delete the labels and use a "Text Box" to make and position labels instead.

Match the diagram to your message. Don't just select the first diagram you see and squeeze your ideas into it.

- *Consider what the diagram means.* For example, save chevrons for items that flow from one to the next, choose a Venn diagram only when items actually overlap, and use circular flows only when the last item leads back to the first.

- *Make shapes bigger, bolder, or central for a reason.* If you are showing a core idea, then position it in the middle or where the audience will look first. If items are similar, then make them appear that way.

- *Check the arrows.* Think what an arrow communicates and resist the urge to use too many of them, unless your message is about chaos or confusion. Downward arrows suggest a somewhat negative message. Curved and diagonal arrows imply more movement and excitement than straight ones; save them for messages about energy, change, cycles, or tension.

3. Photographs add interest.

Photographs can be a wonderful addition to your slide show or deck, but too often they are inserted without enough thought. If a picture is worth 1,000 words, then a bad picture is really worth avoiding. Only choose images that clarify your message.

Finding pictures: Many photos are protected by copyright and you can't use them without permission. However, usable pictures are available if you know where to look.

- *Finding free photos:* Some images are in the "public domain," and you may be able to use them, even for company presentations. Others have a "creative commons" license and may be usable with proper attribution. (See page 148 for more information.) A few sites are dedicated to making free images available; www.morguefile.com is a good place to begin seaching for such images.

- *Purchasing images:* You can buy photos from reasonably priced sources, such as www.dreamstime.com or www.istockphoto.com. You can also purchase CD or DVD collections. Read the terms before you buy. Like free photos, purchased ones may have some limits as to how they can be used.

- *Supplying your own images:* You may be able to use your smartphone or camera to capture an image that communicates your message.

Choosing images: The audience should never wonder why you have included a photo, so pick one that clearly conveys your point. For example, bypass images that look silly or staged, unless you are sending a campy message. Always test the clarity of any image you choose; see how it projects on a screen or prints on a deck page.

Altering photos: If necessary, alter a picture so it looks better on your slide or page. If you resize it, keep the proportions the same so that you don't stretch or squish the image. If the colors aren't right, switch to grayscale or use picture-editing software to adjust them. As shown on the next page, you can also crop a photo to change its shape or focal point. If the image doesn't include letters or numbers, in most cases, you can also flip it.

Example: photograph that can be cropped and flipped

Positioning photos: Pictures grab attention so position them carefully. With slide shows, filling the whole screen with a photo can be very powerful; place it on a black background so nothing but the image projects on the screen. When grouping photos, arrange them so they look balanced; align their edges or create a montage with a primary focus (one picture that stands out because of its color, size, or shape). As shown below, also make sure any photo you include guides a viewer's eyes in the right direction.

ALTERING AND POSITIONING PHOTOGRAPHS

Crop images to adjust shape.
You can crop photos (or digitally snip their edges) to make two photos the same shape, unless their backgrounds or layouts prevent you from doing so.

Position photos carefully.
If a picture directs attention to the left or right, have it face text rather than the edge of the slide or page. (The snail is now climbing toward this text, whereas the scissors are headed toward the text about cropping.)

Photos: morguefile.com (Jane Sawyer, left, and Lisa Solonynko, right)

Capturing interest with other options: There are many other ways to add visual interest. You can include drawings, ranging from an image supplied by an artist to a simple one you add yourself. Using maps is another option; they can show where a global corporation has opened offices or how to find a local restaurant. If they are appropriate, cartoons can add a bit of humor. With slides, you can add motion and sound by using video clips.

4. Animation clarifies complex slides.

"Animation" is the PowerPoint tool that allows you to build—or systematically reveal—one point or image at a time. By using animation, you control the flow of information, which will prevent audience members from becoming confused or reading ahead. Avoid the temptation to create flashing arrows, flying bullets, or pointless motion between slides. Instead, select simple options such as "Appear" or one that focuses attention on your point and not the movement on the screen.

- *Build lines of text.* Your audience will read ahead. However, you can use animation and dimmed text to focus their attention on the current point. For example, with bullet lists, use animation when the text line acts like a topic sentence, listing a point you plan to talk about in great detail; however, don't use it for quick lists where you won't be adding content to what's on the slide. If you build your agenda slide, it will force you to slow down and help your audience focus on your important points.

- *Build complex charts.* Adding animation can help the audience understand your point. For example, with a bubble chart, you might begin with the title and axes, making sure the comparisons are clear. Next you might add the featured bubble and discuss its placement and size. Finally, you could add other bubbles, perhaps a quadrant at a time, pointing out what you want the audience to see.

- *Add layers to diagrams.* If a diagram is complex, then build it. For example, show the foundation of a pyramid diagram, then dim the base's color and add new layers, until you reach the top.

- *Avoid distracting transitions.* "Transitions" are the movement from one slide to the next. Spinning wheels and dissolving checkerboards are a distraction as are transitions that include silly sounds. Unless you are adding movement to emphasize your message, it's usually better to let slides simply appear on the screen.

5. Text charts list important details.

Although some image-driven slides don't include bullet lists, they are still common on traditional slides and deck pages. When you use visuals that rely on words, do your best to (1) keep them simple, (2) ensure that lists have parallel structure, (3) fine-tune the formatting, and (4) add a visual flourish.

Keep slides exceptionally simple. A great debate rages about how many words should be on a slide. Some experts have banned bullet points. Others suggest limiting the number of bullet points on a slide and the length of the text lines.

One thing isn't a debate: people can't read and listen to words simultaneously. When your audience is reading a list, they're not listening to you. Keeping text to a minimum alleviates this problem, which is why everyone also agrees that loading up your visuals with text is a terrible idea.

How many words are too many?

- The six-word title is Calibri.
- The text uses the same font.
- Calibri's small "x-height" means you would choose one of the larger text sizes, such as 30-point text.
- Even so, about 10 words would fit on the longer lines of text, making them a bit difficult to read.
- Once the seventh line of text is added, this slide looks overloaded.
- If we remind you to adjust the line spacing and to avoid long bullets that wrap to a third line, then we just made a truly bad slide even worse.

Keep deck pages simple. You can put more words on a deck page than a slide, but the more you use, the harder it will be to keep your presentation from turning into a group reading session. Decks viewed during a presentation should feature images rather than words.

To keep your text visuals simple, consider the following suggestions:

- *Be concise.* Search for simple edits like those below:

Wordy phrase	Simpler language
in order to	to
each and every member	members
continue to advocate for	push for
be cognizant of	know
utilize	use

- *Maintain stand-alone sense.* Although you want to simplify bullet lists, you don't want to cut so much that they no longer make stand-alone sense as explained on page 85.

Lacks stand-alone sense	Makes stand-alone sense
• Jobs	• High-paying, local jobs
• Energy	• Carbon-free, safe energy
• Subsidies	• Long-term, federal subsidies

- *Switch to active voice.* Active voice relies on strong verbs such as "decide" and "create," while passive voice softens the tone, using weaker verbs such as "is" and "might be." For example, assume a title reads, "Additional learning will result from the continued use of behavior scan testing." Switched to active voice, this title claims, "Behavior scan testing assists our research." You might be able to cut many words on your deck pages by using more active voice. To learn more, download one of the plain language guides listed on page 149.

- *Limit your use of subpoints.* Don't create subpoints for your subpoints. Once a bullet list looks more like an outline than a list, it loses even more visual appeal.

Use parallel structure. Look at how you have phrased your title and examine the words listed below it. To be clear, lists need to use parallel structure—which includes both grammatical and conceptual parallelism.

- *Grammatical parallelism:* If the first words of all the items on your list use the same part of speech (for example, all nouns or all action verbs), then your job will be easier; you are less likely to stumble when you move to a new point if each line of text begins the same way.

Not grammatically parallel	*Grammatically parallel*
• Checking health-care plans	• Check health-care plans
• Comparison of dental plans	• Compare dental plans
• About pension funds	• Review pension funds

• *Conceptual parallelism:* Sometimes the main idea gets combined with lesser points and the real title for your slide isn't in bold letters at the top; instead, you find it tucked away at the bottom of a list. Or maybe some of the points in your list don't seem to match the title. Professor Joann Yates coined the term "conceptual parallelism" to refer to times when subpoints and main points don't go together. In the following example, the problem becomes clear as soon as you realize pension funds don't have anything to do with health care:

Not conceptually parallel	*Conceptually parallel*
Learn About Health Care	**Learn About Your Benefits**
• Check health-care plans.	• Check health and dental plans.
• Compare dental plans.	• Review pension funds.
• Review pension funds.	

Fine-tune the formatting. Before you start adding text, turn off the features that automatically downsize title and text fonts to make them fit in their placeholders:

- *In older versions of PowerPoint,* the "Autofit" features are in the "Tools" menu.

- *In the 2007 version,* click on the "Office Button" in the upper-left corner of the screen. At the bottom of the menu, you will find "PowerPoint Options." From there, click on "Proofing," and then "Autocorrect Options." Make sure the "Autofit Title Text to Placeholder" and "Autofit Body Text to Placeholder" choices are not checked.

- *In the 2010 version,* Look at the top of the screen and click the small, black, downward arrow to find "PowerPoint Options." Select "Proofing," then click on "Autocorrect Options." Make sure the "Autofit" options are not checked.

Once you are ready to insert text, you have formatting choices to make, in addition to those you made for the Slide Master. Think about how you will use capital letters, break long lines of text, and highlight important information.

- *Consider your use of case.* For titles, you have two options. You can use title case, which capitalizes the first letter of each word. Or you can use sentence case, which only capitalizes the first letter of the first word. If you centered your titles, then title case tends to look better. With left-justified titles, we often prefer sentence case. For bullet lists, chose either sentence case or lower case; title case will make your text lines much harder to read. If you plan to use lower case, then turn off the autocorrect feature that capitalizes the first word in a line of text.

- *Wrap lines of text so they look balanced.* Try not to leave a single word by itself on a line. Instead, divide the title or text line in a way that makes sense, based on the content. If the right margin of a long quote looks uneven, try to even it by breaking lines of text. To do so, position the cursor where you want the line to end, then hold down the "Shift" and "Enter" keys.

- *Use simple highlighting options.* If you decide to highlight a word or line, do so with care. Too much boldface text will make nothing stand out; italics will look less dramatic, but will be hard to read if used for large blocks of text. Placing words vertically or curving them with "Word Art" won't help readability either. Finally, save all capital letters for labels or single words, using them SPARINGLY.

Add a visual flourish. Some people disguise their bullet lists by enclosing each point in a shape or putting the whole list in a box. You can also put a photograph next to a list, as long as the image directs attention toward the text. The following slide images show how a list can become a bit more visual.

Plain list	*More visual version*
Four Steps to Four Stars	**Four Steps to Four Stars**
• Listening to our guests	Listening Providing
• Providing service as a team	to our guests service as a team
• Creating a sense of luxury	
• Enhancing our reputation	Enhancing Creating
	our reputation a sense of luxury

IV. EDIT YOUR EFFORTS.

Make sure your visuals have a clear structure, use color and graphics effectively, and print or project without errors.

I. Verify that the structure is clear.

To check the structure, focus on your preview visual. In a slide show, you may want to repeat this slide between each section of your talk. In a deck, you might want to include section visuals that are linked to the table of contents. In complex slide shows or decks, you might also want to insert trackers to reinforce the structure.

Repeating the preview slide: Copy and insert the preview slide before each section, highlighting the section that comes next.

Examples of highlighted preview visuals

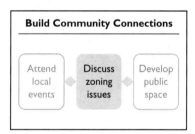

Adding trackers: A tracker is a word or symbol that links a visual to the correct section. Make trackers small, but visible.

Tracker examples: word lower right and symbols at bottom

Northern region showed dramatic improvements	**Eastern region faces multiple challenges**
• New hires contributed as trainees	• Turnover rate exceeded 15%
• Expenses held steady	• Travel expenses double
• Profit margins were exceptional	• Profits were disappointing
Northern	N–S–**E**–W

2. Enhance the visual effect.

In addition to editing for structure, check the visual effect of your colors and graphics.

Check your use of color. Look at your diagrams and charts to make sure they are using spot and dimming colors to emphasize the title. The following examples show how color can detract from a diagram's message or enhance the visual effect.

Overuse of color   *Good use of spot color*

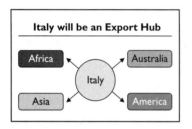   

Use graphics as a "pointer." You can add arrows, lines, circles, or boxes to highlight something on a page. As previously noted, with slides you can also use animation to control the flow of information. Graphics can appear with the slide or they can be added with a click of your mouse; either way, they will guide people's eyes to just the right spot.

Using an arrow or a shape to direct attention

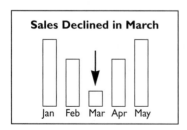

Eliminate chartjunk. To use the term coined by design expert Edward Tufte, eliminate "chartjunk"—those extra design elements that don't contribute to your message. The following examples show how clutter can detract from a pie, bar, and line chart. The table on page 116 lists specific PowerPoint problems that you will want to overcome (such as legends used to indicate the color coding of pie slices, bar segments, or trend lines).

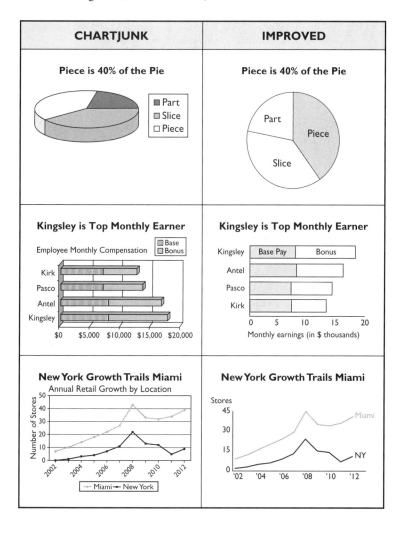

ELIMINATING CHARTJUNK IN POWERPOINT	
Challenge	**Solution**
Avoiding 3D	3D distorts the data so select the 2D views.
Deleting legends	Legends slow down the viewer. Cut them from pie, line, and bar charts (and complex column charts if possible). In recent PowerPoint versions, use legend button on chart layout ribbon to choose "None." In earlier versions, click twice on the legend after it is already in the chart, then right click to delete it.
Labeling chart elements	Use the "Text Box" to make labels. Position them with arrow keys and "Align" tools. Place labels on or near pie slices, next to or on bars, and near lines.
Simplifying titles and labels	Delete repetitive titles. Eliminate extra zeros by adding "thousands" or "millions" to axis label instead. When data points are clearly labeled (for example, "May," "June," "July"), cut needless axis labels such as "Months."
Avoiding vertical column labels	Avoid vertical and angled labels under columns by making columns wider, not using too many columns, and using brief labels ("9/14" for "September 2014").
Changing width of columns/bars	To increase their default width, edit the "Data Series," using the option that lets you make the "Gap Width" smaller.
Improving line charts	Click on the line chart, then right click on the trend line and go to "Format Data Series," where you can choose the line's color, increase its width, and cut "Data Markers"—the little squares, triangles, or circles that appear on the trend line.
Cutting borders and extra lines	Eliminate the border or background that appears around the chart. Cut grid lines not needed to clarify meaning; delete small lines or "tick marks" jutting out from each axis.
Adjusting chart colors	Click on the pie chart; then click on a pie slice. Next, right click on the pie slice to recolor it. Use spot color for key slice and dimming option for less important ones. Recolor lines, bars, and columns the same way.
Positioning slices and bars	Insert data in an order that makes sense based on the message. Make the key pie slice appear at 12 o'clock position; make sure bars are arranged in a logical way.

3. Proof and proof again.

Finally, check for consistency and correctness. You want to maintain consistent phrasing, document your sources, and confirm that your slides and pages are error-free.

Maintain consistent phrasing. Use the same wording on your slides and pages that you did on your preview visual. For example, if you list "financial projections" on your preview slide, don't switch to "spreadsheet analysis" on the supporting visual. Similarly, if using trackers, link them to your preview. For instance, if you wrote "Northern Region" in the table of contents and used the word "Northern" as a tracker, the connection would be clear. However, if "Mid-Atlantic Region" was listed in the preview, with the word "Eastern" used as its tracker, the connection wouldn't be so obvious.

Document your sources. If you are using a chart, cite any numbers that come from outside the organization. If you don't know the source, then you shouldn't be using the data. Similarly, if you use an expert's words, identify them as that person's ideas and not your own. On projected visuals, use limited citations, perhaps just noting the publication or the author's last name. On decks, you can include more detail. You might even want to include a bibliography in the appendix. You'll find a comprehensive reference for citing sources at http://library.hbs.edu/guides/citationguide.pdf.

Check for errors. One of the easiest ways to allow little mistakes to creep into your visuals is to proof them, make last-minute changes, and fail to proof them again.

- *Don't rely on the spell-checker.* Lots of mistakes get caught with this tool, but many others are missed. Print your work; it's easier to find errors on a printed page than on your computer screen.
- *Check the numbers one more time.* Make sure you didn't transpose any digits when you entered data. In a deck, check page numbers. Be sure the table of contents matches the actual pages and there isn't a page missing in anyone's deck.
- *Test the animation and colors in a slide show.* Run through the slide show and make sure items appear the way you intended. As soon as possible, test your colors on the big screen.

CHAPTER 6 OUTLINE

I. ANALYZE YOUR NONVERBAL STYLE.
   1. Body position and movement
   2. Hand and arm gestures
   3. Eye contact and facial expression
   4. Vocal traits
   5. Space and objects around you

II. PRACTICE YOUR DELIVERY.
   1. Get comfortable with the content and timing.
   2. Rehearse with your slides.
   3. Prepare for deck presentations.
   4. Prepare for online presentations.

III. MANAGE YOUR NERVOUS SYMPTOMS.
   1. General techniques
   2. Physical techniques
   3. Mental techniques
   4. Last-minute tips

CHAPTER 6

Refine Your Nonverbal Delivery

The third part of implementation focuses on your nonverbal skills—how you look and sound to your audience. We all know that nonverbal elements are crucial to a presentation's success. Even so, "perfect" delivery is not necessary. In fact, it's not even possible since different people prefer different delivery styles. What's most important is being authentic and sincere, not artificial and over-rehearsed.

Although you always want to look and sound natural, you will want to adapt your delivery to the formality of the situation. With practice, you should be able to develop a range of effective delivery behaviors that all look and sound like you. As you work on your delivery, use the suggestions in this chapter to (1) analyze your non-verbal style, (2) practice your delivery, and (3) manage your nervous symptoms.

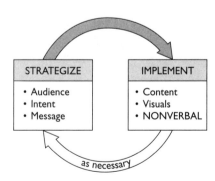

STRATEGIZE
• Audience
• Intent
• Message

IMPLEMENT
• Content
• Visuals
• NONVERBAL

as necessary

I. ANALYZE YOUR NONVERBAL STYLE.

Many nonverbal elements affect your delivery. Some are your own behaviors, such as your gesturing habits and facial expression. You can observe them by watching a recording of yourself or rehearsing in front of a mirror. Other nonverbal elements are separate from you, such as the lighting in the room and the distance between you and your audience. All of these nonverbal behaviors are situational: they vary by personality, place, audience, and culture.

1. Body position and movement

A solid stance, upright posture, and purposeful movement communicate confidence. Position your body and move in ways that make you look natural as well as poised.

Distracting positions are often obvious from the start of a presentation. Where you position your legs and feet affects your whole body and influences how you move.

- *The informal "hip sit":* If you rest your weight on one leg or "park on your hip," your stance will look informal. The distractions begin when your legs get tired: if you switch back and forth, from one leg to the other, the unintended motion can attract unwanted attention.

- *Problematic foot placement:* Standing with your feet too far apart makes you look like a ranch hand doing the "cowpoke straddle." However, placing them too close together makes you look submissive. Be sure to check your toes: if they are pointed away from your heels, in a "duck stance," you may look as if you are waddling when you walk.

- *Leaning troubles:* Leaning positions such as the "podium clutch" and "table lean" leave your legs and feet free to do distracting things— such as swing, wrap, twist, or tap.

- *Moving mistakes:* Watch for distracting motion, such as bouncing, rocking, and pacing. Also avoid taking single steps up and back or side to side. Such repetitive, purposeless motion distracts the audience.

- *Sloppy sitting:* Check how people sit around a conference table. Slouching doesn't look professional. Swiveling soon gets distracting.

Effective formal positions usually involve standing; being above your audience creates a more formal environment than being seated at the same level. Standing on a stage, behind a podium, creates an exceptionally formal look. But even when you are standing in front of a small group, you will want to use a solid opening stance and combine it with movement that is appropriate for the situation.

- *Position your legs and feet formally.* To create a formal opening stance: (1) place your feet about shoulder-width apart, rather than very close together or far apart; (2) distribute your weight evenly, using both legs equally for support; (3) divide your weight between your heels and the balls of your feet; (4) make sure your feet are straight and not in "duck" position; and (5) don't lock your knees. This position tends to feel awkward until you get used to it, but it looks good and prevents unintended movement.

- *Return to the formal stance after you move.* In formal situations, it's fine to move for a reason—to emphasize a point on your visual aid, for example, or to move closer to the audience to signal that you are seeking questions. Just make sure your feet are in the formal position described earlier, once you have finished moving.

Effective informal positions include more options. For example, you can signal that you want to create an informal exchange by leaning momentarily against a table or using a more casual posture. You might also choose to present from a chair.

Environmental factors influence where you stand and how you move: (1) *Room size* is one consideration. For example, in a large room, one effective way to use movement is to walk to a new place in the room to indicate that you are beginning a new section of your talk. (2) *Seating arrangements* may also be a factor. For example, in a "U-shaped" arrangement, you don't want to spend too much time in the center of the room since people on the side will only have a view of your back.

Personal style also affects movement. Some people have lots of energy and prefer to move around the room; they need to be careful not to walk too much and to remain still at times, giving the audience a break from all that motion. Other presenters prefer to stay in one place, sometimes seeking safety behind a podium; they may want to walk to a new place, when appropriate, to add variety to their delivery.

2. Hand and arm gestures

When standing, many presenters feel awkward: they don't know where to put their hands, and their arms suddenly feel too long. To use your hands and arms effectively, we suggest you (1) discover your natural gesturing style, (2) avoid distracting gestures, (3) use conversational patterns, and (4) adapt to the situation.

Discover your natural gesturing style. To do so, get a sense of your gesturing habits in various situations, such as when you are talking at a cocktail party or across a dinner table. Ask people who know you to comment on how often you gesture and which gestures you tend to use. Inquire about the size of your gestures, and find out about any distracting arm, hand, or finger habits. Even better, arrange to be recorded so you can see an example of your gesturing style for yourself.

Avoid distracting gestures. Once you learn about your tendencies, you will want to eliminate distracting gestures and avoid overusing your favorites. Some small, repetitive gestures are signs of stress. These nervous fidgets include touching your hair, rubbing your face, and twisting your ring, just to describe a few. In addition, many hand and arm positions have descriptive or humorous names; they tend to send the wrong nonverbal message.

- *The commander* places her hands on her hips.
- *The chilly presenter* crosses his arms over his chest.
- *The gun-shot victim* clings to her upper arm with one hand.
- *The armless presenter* leaves his hands behind his back.
- *The pocket jingler* puts a hand in her pocket, shaking keys and coins.
- *The clutcher* grasps a pen or pointer and never puts the object down.
- *The slapper* makes noise as he hits his palms against his thighs.
- *The Garden of Eden presenter* clasps her hands in front of her, where a fig leaf would be.

Use conversational patterns. Aside from avoiding distracting gestures, you want your gesturing style as a speaker to match the style you use in conversations. If possible, you also want to use some gestures that reinforce your points.

- *Emphasize your message.* Some gestures go along with your verbal content, adding nonverbal reinforcement to your message. For example, if you are "balancing two issues," your palms might be turned up, alternately moving up and down to simulate a scale. Try not to force such gestures. The best emphatic gestures are those you really tend to use.

- *Avoid extremes.* Most of your gestures should be below your face and above your waist. Watch for extremes: if you use lots of huge gestures that extend down to your knees and over your head, you may look more like a cheerleader than a business presenter. On the other hand, if you keep your hands at your sides and use only tiny movements, you may resemble a flapping penguin.

- *Point appropriately.* Reserve pointing for visual aids, not for people. Or try "friendly pointing" that uses your whole hand, keeping your palm sidewise or tilted slightly up and your fingers together.

- *Refine, but don't obsess.* Remember, you don't need to be perfect. You might fidget once, slap your thigh, overuse your favorite gesture, and still accomplish your presentation objective. Practice to refine your gesturing style, but don't obsess about it.

Adapt to the situation. Although you want them to be natural, your gestures should also be influenced by the environment and the expectations of the audience.

- *Consider room size.* In a large room, gestures can be big and still look appropriate; however, speaking in a small space or appearing on a TV screen requires smaller gestures.

- *Think about your audience.* Some people like presenters who gesture often. Others prefer limited gesturing. You can't please everyone, so usually it's best to use your own style. However, if you see that people are staring at your hands, perhaps you'll want to scale back some of your gesturing. Similarly, if you tend to look a bit too formal, adding a few gestures, especially friendly "palms up" gestures, can make your style seem less rigid.

- *Consider cultural norms.* In some cultures, expansive gestures are common, while in other cultures gesturing tends to be far more restrained. One of the most important cultural differences to consider involves hand signals that stand on their own. What you use to show "OK" may not mean "everything is all right" in some cultures. Similarly, the "thumbs up" and "stop" signals have various meanings. Be very careful when using such gestures in cross-cultural situations; you don't want to unintentionally send an insulting or even vulgar message.

3. Eye contact and facial expression

Your face plays a crucial role in your nonverbal delivery style: your eye contact connects you to your audience, and your face communicates interest, confidence, and enthusiasm.

Eye contact: Most U.S. business audiences want you to "look them in the eye"—a mark of honesty and confidence according to cultural norms. Here are some tips to assist you as you use eye contact to connect with your audience:

- *Find a friendly face.* If you are nervous, making eye contact with a supportive person might actually calm you down. The smiles and nods you see from the friendly face can help you get through the difficult parts of your presentation and boost your confidence.

- *Have little conversations.* Imagine you are speaking to one person at a time so you will feel less intimidated by a large audience and be able to develop a more natural delivery style.

- *Look long enough to complete a thought.* You don't want to stare. But you don't want your eye contact to be darting. Therefore, look at a person's whole face—not just the pupils—and look long enough to complete a thought or register a reaction.

- *Locate influential audience members.* When delivering a persuasive presentation, check the reactions of the decision makers and other people with influence. However, don't focus on these people to the extent that others may feel excluded.

- *Use your body as you make eye contact.* In a wide room, if you move only your head from one side to the other, the audience will begin to feel as if they are watching you watch a tennis match. To overcome this problem, turn more than just your neck and head when you look from side to side and connect with people sitting in the middle as you move your eyes across the room.

- *Make adjustments for large audiences.* If you are speaking before a crowd of hundreds, try to find one person in each section of the audience to use as an anchor point for your eye contact. If you then start looking at people sitting around these anchors, you can be sure you aren't ignoring part of the audience. When lighting prevents you from seeing anyone, you still need to give the appearance of making eye contact throughout the room.

Facial expression: What the audience sees on your face will affect how they hear your message. Try to avoid the stony, deadpan expression of ineffective speakers. Instead, relax your face and use natural expressions that are appropriate for your message.

- *Use conversational expression.* Like gesturing, facial expression is very speaker specific. Use your natural expressions to connect with the audience.
- *Smile when appropriate.* Conversational facial expression does not mean you have to smile all the time. For example, you might want to smile when you introduce yourself, but avoid smiling out of nervousness or when discussing sad or serious topics.
- *Interact with the audience.* Try the technique of looking at someone in the audience with "appropriate" facial expression and mirror the look on that person's face. For example, if you want to remember to smile, look at a friendly face; that person's smile might help you express one of your own.

4. Vocal traits

Your voice should sound natural and interesting. To achieve this sound, avoid reading or memorizing. Reading causes most people to stumble over words and use unnatural vocal patterns. Memorizing leads to an artificial style because it usually sounds rehearsed. Instead, use a natural-sounding style. To do so, become aware of the elements that make up your vocal image, such as volume, rate, inflection, and enunciation. You'll want to vary the first three and enunciate in a way that suits the formality of the situation.

Volume: Your volume is determined by how loudly or softly you speak. You need to be loud enough for everyone to hear you, but you don't want to overwhelm people with sound. Many people can't accurately assess their volume, so it's a good idea to go to the presentation room ahead of time with a friend; ask this person to stand in the back so you can test your volume. If you have a booming voice, you may want to lower the sound level a bit. If your volume is low, know that your voice will be even harder to hear once people fill the room. Since too little volume, rather than too much, tends to be an issue for many speakers, here are some tips to make sure you can be heard:

- *Speak to the back row.* If you have a soft, hard-to-hear voice, begin by speaking to the person farthest away from you and try not to let this volume drop.

- *Avoid vocal strain.* Learn how to increase volume without creating vocal strain. Begin by pretending that you are perched on a balcony, with the audience sitting below. When you attempt to send your voice downward, you will produce sound by pushing from your diaphragm rather than your throat. Your volume will increase, but you won't sound as if you are shouting. Even better, you won't strain your vocal cords.

- *Listen for volume drops.* Volume sometimes drops to inaudible levels in two situations: (1) *At the end of sentences:* If your voice trails off at the end of sentences, try pausing as you complete a thought; take in enough air to keep your volume strong all the way to the end of the sentence. (2) *As you introduce a new slide:* If people can't hear you when you put up a new slide, either talk to the people in the back row or pause if you need to turn away to put up a new visual.

- *Vary volume.* If you say some words or phrases with extra volume, you can emphasize them. For speakers with loud voices, sometimes lowering the sound level can also get attention.

- *Test the microphone.* If a microphone is creating volume for you, practice with it. You won't want to get too close or you'll hear a horrible screeching sound.

Rate: Your rate involves the speed of your delivery—how quickly or slowly you say your words and how and when you insert pauses.

- *Slow down if you talk too fast.* When some speakers feel anxious or excited, they tend to speak faster than usual. If you are one of these fast talkers, you will want to slow your pace when you are presenting. Try rehearsing your presentation at an artificially slow rate; as you present, you will recall this rehearsal rate and have an easier time slowing down.

- *Add pauses.* One of the best ways to slow your overall rate is to use more pauses. To do so, try to get comfortable with silence. Add an audible pause at the end of a sentence. Use this time to breathe deeply before speaking again. Pause briefly for commas. And try inserting a pause before and after an important message. It will make your point stand out.

- *Speed up if you talk too slowly.* If you speak at a very slow rate, try to speed up at times, for instance, when the material is simple. You might also try to vary other elements of your voice, such as inflection, to make your voice sound lively.

- *Adjust for cultural differences.* (1) *Alter your rate,* so it is appropriate for the culture. For example, in the northeastern region of the United States, a fairly rapid rate is the norm; however, in the South, most people speak more slowly. (2) *Consider your accent:* if your accent isn't familiar to your audience, then slow down, especially at the beginning, so people can get used to your speech patterns. (3) *Remember non-native speakers:* slow down and make other adjustments as noted on page 10 to help listeners who are learning the language.

Inflection: We use the word "inflection" to refer to speaking with variation in your pitch.

- *Speak with expressiveness and enthusiasm,* in a warm, pleasant tone, with enough variety to create a lively and energetic delivery.

- *Avoid speaking in a monotone.* The opposite of effective inflection is a dull, robotic monotone that makes you sound as if you are bored. To improve a monotone voice, try saying long lists of words or numbers, using your voice to say some items with a high note and others with a low note. Once you've mastered making a list sound intriguing, you can then decide which messages in your presentation need the same sort of vocal emphasis.

- *Add low notes to a high-pitched voice.* Deep voices tend to be heard as more authoritative than higher-pitched ones. So, if you have a very high voice, you will want to learn how to lower your pitch and eliminate any shrill-sounding tones. To do so, practice diaphragmatic breathing as explained on page 139.

- *Avoid turning statements into questions.* When you make a statement, your voice goes down at the end of the sentence. When you ask a question, you use upward inflection. Some people unintentionally turn statements into questions, ending far too many sentences on a high note, which can make them sound unsure of themselves and decrease their credibility. To avoid this problem, practice driving inflection downward at the end of sentences.

Enunciation: Also known as "articulation," enunciation refers to how clearly you say your words. Whether you enunciate formally or informally should depend on the nature of your presentation.

- *To use formal enunciation,* you need to speak carefully, saying all your consonants and making sure your vowels are heard. Avoid dropping final letters (so that "talking" becomes "talkin") or squeezing words together (so that "going to" sounds like "gunna").

- *In less formal situations,* using such careful enunciation can make you sound stiff. While you do want to make sure your words can be understood, you don't need to use such precise articulation. In these cases, you can use contractions, replacing "do not" with "don't" and "you will" with "you'll" to create a breezier style.

- *To avoid stumbling over words,* in either formal or informal situations, identify the words that cause you trouble. For example, perhaps the word "similarly" is hard for you to say. If so, breathe before you use this word and think about each syllable as you say it. Sometimes you can rely on a synonym, perhaps using "likewise" to make your job easier.

Filler words and sounds: These verbal pauses are words and sounds that creep into your speech. Along with stutters, stumbles, and poor enunciation, they hurt the smoothness of your delivery. Some common fillers are "uh," "er," "um," and "you know." Using a few "ums" is natural for many speakers; if used only occasionally, they are not a problem. However, if used repeatedly, these words and sounds can become a distraction.

- *Add pauses to cut back on filler words and sounds.* If you overuse fillers, try to add pauses to replace some of them. Also attempt to become comfortable with silence; some people insert fillers because the lack of sound bothers them.

- *Listen for advanced filler words.* Some speakers have developed what communication expert Joann Baney calls "advanced filler words." These speakers create amazingly long compound, complex sentences by avoiding pauses and inserting words such as "and" or "so." While it's fine to start a sentence with a "so" or "and," doing it too often may affect your breathing.

- *Avoid meaningless phrases.* Some people use the same words so often that people begin to notice. Needless phrases such as "to be honest," may make a speaker sound less than honest. Similarly, "as a matter of fact," can be omitted and replaced with the fact.

5. Space and objects around you

Other nonverbal elements have to do with the space and objects around you. All of them will affect your delivery.

Space: Check out the size and shape of the room, its furnishings, and the distance between you and the audience.

- *Consider the seating arrangement.* Straight lines of chairs create a formal environment. On the other hand, a horseshoe or U-shape arrangement encourages participation and creates a less formal atmosphere. Even the shape of a table matters; for instance, presenting at a round table seems less formal than choosing to sit at the head of a long, rectangular one.

- *Factor in height and distance.* The higher you are in relationship to your audience, the more formal the atmosphere you establish nonverbally. Therefore, the most formal presentations might be delivered from a stage or platform. In a semiformal situation, you might stand while the audience sits. To make a situation even less formal, you might sit with your audience at a table or in a circle of chairs. Distance is also linked to formality. The farther you are away from the audience, the more formal you will appear.

Objects: Think also about the objects you choose to have around you, including what you wear.

- *Objects between you and the audience:* To increase formality, use objects (such as a podium or table) to separate yourself from your audience. To decrease formality, don't place objects between yourself and the audience.

- *Visual aids:* Interacting with your visual aids affects your delivery as detailed on pages 132–134. If used poorly, your visuals can become an unintended barrier between you and the audience.

- *Dress:* Think about the audience's expectations and choose apparel that is right for the occasion, the organization, and the culture. For instance, what is appropriate to fashion editors may be totally unacceptable to investment bankers. Similarly, a suit that works great for an interview may look out of place on casual Friday. Avoid apparel that draws too much attention—such as exaggerated, dangling jewelry or loud, flashy ties. Dress to project the image you want to create, one that will enhance your credibility.

II. PRACTICE YOUR DELIVERY.

Use the rehearsal techniques covered in this section to prepare for various types of presentations.

1. Get comfortable with the content and timing.

Put together limited notes and rehearse out loud to become aware of content, timing, and nonverbal issues.

Prepare limited notes. If you organized your presentation with an outline, you can easily turn that outline into notes. If you used an idea chart or a storyboard, then translate it into a simple outline.

- *Do not write complete sentences.* Instead, use very short phrases for each point or subpoint.
- *Use large lettering and lots of white space* so your notes are uncluttered and easy to read.
- *Save your outlined notes.* These notes will be helpful reminders when you want to talk through your content informally. In addition, should your laptop fail or your deck disappear, this outline will enable you to practice or present without your visuals.

"Own" your content. When time allows, go through the content multiple times with colleagues or friends. It's often useful to talk about the subject with people who know little about it. Once you can explain a point in different ways—without using the exact same words—you've made that point your own. Owning your content will enable you to access it easily and naturally.

Connect your notes to your slides. If you are giving a stand-up slide presentation, use "Notepage" and "Presenter View."

- *Create "Notepages."* Use the "Notepage" feature in PowerPoint to link the short phrases in your outlined notes to the corresponding visuals you created in PowerPoint. When you print these pages, you will see your notes under the images of your slides.
- *Check the "Presenter View."* Set your laptop up as you would if you were projecting slides, but rather than choosing "Slideshow View" opt for "Presenter View." When you present, your audience will see the notes-free, projected version, while you will see the slide image and notes on your screen.

Rehearse your presentation. Once you have your notes, you are ready to rehearse. If the material is complicated and new, you will likely need to run through it more than once, timing yourself to ensure that you won't run overtime. If your presentation is similar to one you've given before, you may only need to practice your opening, your closing, and the transitions between sections.

- *Rehearse out loud.* In all cases, practice out loud. Knowing your content is not the same as saying it. So, don't just read over your notes; instead say the material out loud, using the vocal traits you want to use on the day of your talk.

- *Rehearse the way you'll present.* If you will be standing when you speak, then get on your feet when you rehearse; if you will be sitting when you present, then sit down when you practice.

- *Rehearse onsite.* If possible, rehearse in the place where you will present so you will become comfortable with the environment.

- *Make adjustments.* An initial rehearsal will point out where your structure is weak, if you are missing transitions, and if you have too much material. In following rehearsals, focus on polishing your nonverbal skills and becoming comfortable with your visual aids.

Time a rehearsal. Running overtime can annoy your audience and undercut your credibility. Only by practicing your entire presentation out loud, can you effectively check your timing. If you plan to use visual aids, practice showing them during your timed rehearsal.

- *Time each section.* If you are rehearsing on your own, practice each section by itself and note how long it takes. Or better yet, record your rehearsal so you will be able to document the length of each section. As another option, ask someone to attend your rehearsal and time the various sections of your talk. With this information, you can make better choices about how to cut material.

- *Plan to finish early.* If your rehearsal reveals that you will end almost exactly on time, you still need to make cuts. Factor in the time you will need to respond to questions and the time the audience will need to understand your visual aids.

- *Decide how to make additional cuts.* Prepare to adjust timing further, if necessary, during your presentation. If you run short on time, do not rush through your points. Instead, plan to cut details and empha-size key messages.

2. Rehearse with your slides.

As soon as possible, incorporate your slides into your rehearsals. Practice until you can gracefully integrate them into your talk.

Link what they'll see to what you'll say. Even well-designed slides don't speak for themselves. It's your job to help them communicate your message.

- *Know how you'll cue the audience.* You'll need to tell people where to look, show them, or do both. Consider using animation to direct people's eyes to the right place on the screen.

- *Practice introducing and building each slide.* Figure out what you'll say before and as a new slide appears on the screen. For example, you might ask: "So what is our main recommendation?" Then, pause before advancing to the next slide, allowing your audience to see it, before saying, "We need to equip our entire sales force with tablets." Also consider what you'll say as items appear or exit from the screen.

- *Give extra attention to complex images.* Practice introducing the main idea and carefully explaining the meaning of any symbols, colors, axes, or labels you have used.

- *Take your time.* As you become familiar with the content on your slides, it will seem natural to speed up as you talk about them, but don't. Remember that every slide will be new to your audience; they'll need plenty of time to process what you project on the screen.

Anticipate visual distractions. You'll want to get rid of old slides and become comfortable *not* looking at your visuals. What's on the screen shouldn't become a distraction.

- *Eliminate old news.* Once you are done with an image, plan to remove it. Avoid going into detail about a new idea while everyone is looking at an old slide. To take attention away from the screen, insert a plain black slide into your slide show or use the blank screen command on your remote (or the "B" key on your keyboard). When you make the screen unobtrusive, the audience's attention should go back to you.

- *Be ready to look at the audience.* For a presenter, slides can become eye-contact magnets, so don't let them disconnect you from your audience. If you look over your shoulder at the screen or stare at your laptop, you won't be communicating with people; you'll be talking to your slides. Ideally, you will become so comfortable with your slides that you need to do little more than glance at them.

- *Insert extra slides at the end.* Either make extra copies of your final slide or insert several black slides at the end of your slide show to make sure an extra click on the remote won't send you out of slideshow mode and back to the PowerPoint program. Endings are important. Guarantee that your closing message—and not the PowerPoint program—will have the spotlight.

Practice in the room. Whenever possible, check out the room and the equipment well before you'll be presenting.

- *Become familiar with the equipment.* Set up all the equipment so you won't be searching for ports and switches or testing lighting options while the audience watches. Remember to practice with the remote so you can go forward, backward, and fade the screen to black.

- *Set up the computer.* Your slideshow will run faster from your laptop or the console PC than it will from a memory stick. If using your laptop, be sure you turn off screen savers and the power-saving mode. If using "Presenter View," make sure your notes are easily visible from where you plan to stand.

- *Check your slide show from the back row.* Verify that everything is visible and that the colors are projecting the way you intended. If you embedded a video clip into your slideshow, play it to make sure it runs smoothly and the volume is appropriate for the room.

3. Prepare for deck presentations.

Deck presentations pose a different set of issues than stand-up slide presentations. You'll need to work hard to keep everyone focused on the same page.

Practice how you'll open. Plan to let people know how you want to use the deck. However, remember that deck presentations are supposed to be flexible and interactive. During the presentation you'll need to be responsive to your audience's interests, perhaps by returning to a page or jumping ahead.

- *Explain the deck's purpose.* Clarify how you want to use the deck, whether you intend to go over all of the pages or just some of them. If you have included an appendix, describe what's in it and how the material should be used.

- *Verbally preview the table of contents.* Include a table of contents and review it. For example, you might begin your preview by saying, "As you can see in the table of contents, this deck has four sections...."

Decide what to say about each page. One of the biggest challenges with deck presentations is that since your audience can read faster than you can speak, they may read ahead. Practice the following techniques to keep them on point.

- *Share the main message first.* Begin by highlighting the message in your title. For example, you might say, "As you can see, the Central American division reached its $6 million goal." Tell your audience why the particular point of this page matters.

- *Refer to page numbers.* For example, you might say, "As you'll see on page 12, most of our competition would be larger and far less nimble organizations."

- *Explain colors, symbols, and chart elements.* Since you can't use animation to build complex images, clarify the meaning of colors, axes, and symbols. For example, you might say, "Note the hiring trend for consulting firms, shown as a blue line."

- *Deal with text-heavy pages.* Try to avoid such pages, but if one is inevitable, acknowledge its complexity and remind people they can read it later. Then, summarize it or focus on the take-aways.

- *Link content to individuals.* Search for ways to connect the information on a page to the interests of the audience. When you find a link, you'll be able to use people's name to get their attention. For example, you might say, "Marian, as you can see, the data on this page builds on the numbers you shared in your last deck presentation."

Consider the nonverbal message. Think about where you'll be presenting and how you can look and sound professional.

- *Decide where to sit.* Some experts recommend sitting across from the key decision maker. Others suggest sitting corner-to-corner, sharing the same deck, and pointing to the deck itself.

- *Check out the chair.* When you rehearse, sit in a chair that is similar to the one you'll be using on the day of your talk. Avoid putting your elbows on the table, leaning to one side, tucking your leg under you, or swiveling your chair.

- *Look away from the deck.* Practice until you can paraphrase each page without looking at it.

- *Gesture conversationally.* Don't glue your hands to the table. Use them to gesture naturally. If you tend to fidget, plan to move pens and paper clips out of the way.

4. Prepare for online presentations.

Not all presentations are delivered face to face. Here's how you can prepare if you are presenting online.

- *Become familiar with the equipment.* Rehearse with it by taping and critiquing yourself if possible. Familiarize yourself with the projector and try muting the sound and changing the camera angle.
- *Send your slides* or other electronic documents in advance.
- *Learn what your audience will see on-screen.* With some presentation software, your audience sees exactly what's on your screen, so you can control the progression of slides. With other technologies, however, your audience can scroll through your slides in any way they wish. In these cases, it's important to number your slides so you can say something like, "As you can see on slide 5 . . ."
- *Plan to start early.* Create a "welcome slide" that confirms the meeting details. Opening early will allow your audience to become familiar with the technology while they wait.
- *Provide clues if they cannot see you.* If you are not using a webcam, display a picture of yourself on the welcome slide so your audience can visualize you. You might also break up the tedium of watching slides only by annotating the slides or using a pointer.
- *Enhance your voice.* Excellent vocal delivery is especially important in these kinds of presentations. Speak conversationally, with pauses and inflection. Also speak a bit more slowly, deliberately, and loudly.
- *Stay connected.* When you can't make eye contact, build in questions to make sure people are following and invite their questions to keep them engaged. Otherwise, you won't know if they are texting (or even sleeping!) throughout your talk.
- *Enhance your body language.* When your audience can see you, remember to smile. Talk to the participants as if they were sitting across from you. Look frequently at the webcam, not the screen, so your audience will feel you are making eye contact.

  If you watch TV announcers, you might be able to see how they use nonverbal behaviors that are appropriate on camera. For instance, many use relaxed facial expressions and head movements. Typically, their gestures are small and infrequent, since the screen makes even slight movements seem larger. Don't try to be someone you are not, but do modify your style so it works better on camera.

III. MANAGE YOUR NERVOUS SYMPTOMS.

Nervous feelings are the result of adrenaline pumping through your body. The positive part of an adrenaline rush is that it can increase your energy and prevent your delivery from seeming flat. Many of the other side effects aren't so positive. In this section, we share tips and techniques that can help you manage your nervous symptoms.

I. General techniques

To identify and manage nervous symptoms, consider why you get nervous and what happens when you do. Then, build your confidence by practicing. Also seek feedback that points out what you might improve *and* what you are doing well.

Think about what makes you nervous. Most likely, you are more comfortable in some speaking situations than others. Maybe you feel better when you sit down than you do when you stand. Perhaps a small group filled with friendly faces seems fine, but a huge group of strangers ties your stomach in knots. If you can identify what makes you nervous, you may be able to try a small change that will make a nerve-racking situation seem a little less threatening.

Analyze your symptoms. First, list your symptoms. Then, determine whether the audience will be able to see or hear them. If you experience any of the symptoms in the table below, know that you are not alone and that many of these symptoms can be managed.

ANALYZING COMMON NERVOUS SYMPTOMS		
Visible symptoms	**Audible symptoms**	**Undetectable symptoms**
• Rubbing fingers • Fidgeting with objects • Using very shaky hands • Pacing or rocking • Staring at notes • Darting eye contact • Blushing	• Using many filler words • Speaking too fast • Speaking too softly • Gasping for breath • Stumbling over words • Using noisy gestures (e.g., slapping thighs)	• Pounding heart • Tight chest or shoulders • Queasy stomach • Sweaty palms • Self doubt • Dry mouth • Brief memory loss

- *Visible symptoms:* For symptoms linked to body language, see pages 120–125. Also try some of the techniques on page 138.
- *Audible symptoms:* If your symptoms relate to vocal traits, review pages 125–128. Then look at the vocal advice on page 139.
- *Undetectable symptoms:* Record a rehearsal so you can see and hear for yourself that these symptoms can't be detected. If you have a pounding heart, watch your caffeine intake (since caffeine increases your heart rate) and try the physical and breathing exercises described on pages 138 and 139. You'll find tips for a dry mouth on page 142.

Practice. When it's time to practice, don't take shortcuts. Follow the suggestions in this chapter so you will own the content, have useful notes, be aware of timing issues, and feel confident interacting with your visuals. Ask someone to attend and record a rehearsal so you can practice responding to questions.

Request feedback. Some people give exceptionally useful presentation feedback, while others pile on so many negative, picayune comments that presenters actually end up more nervous than they were before the rehearsal. To get helpful feedback, let people know how you want them to assist.

- *Provide background.* If the people giving you feedback don't know anything about your audience, they won't be able to address content issues, such as whether your use of lingo is appropriate.
- *Explain timing issues.* If your decks are already printed, then have people focus on what you can actually change and not on reordering your content or changing the colors on a chart.
- *Ask what was memorable.* Once you discover what was memorable, you can make sure it was something you really meant to emphasize and learn how you made that message stand out.
- *Find out what you shouldn't change.* Knowing what's effective is as useful as knowing what isn't. For example, an animated voice is interesting and sometimes linked to an active gesturing style. Therefore, even if you think you gesture a little too much, you might not want to reign in your hands, because if you do, your inflection might get reigned in, too.
- *Get information a recording can't give.* When you are being recorded, ask for feedback about things the recording won't tell you. For example, a camera won't reveal whether you projected a visual long enough for someone to understand it.

2. Physical techniques

The following set of techniques is based on the assumption, shared by many athletes and performers, that by relaxing yourself physically, you will calm yourself mentally. Experiment with some of these suggestions until you find one that helps you.

Exercise to control the adrenaline. One way to channel all the nervous energy is to exercise on the day of your talk. Many people calm down following the physical exertion of calisthenics, jogging, tennis, yoga, or another of their preferred athletic activities.

Hold a powerful pose. According to Harvard professor Amy Cuddy, holding your body in an expansive, "high power" pose—for as little as two minutes—alters your hormones, making you feel more powerful and less stressed.

- *Posing before your talk:* Expand your body. For example, put your feet up on a desk and your hands behind your head. After a few minutes, you should be able to feel the effects.

- *Posing while you talk:* The stance we suggest on page 121 should make you feel more powerful than one that draws you in and makes you look as if you are protecting your vital organs (like the fig leaf).

- *Including your face:* Cuddy also acknowledges the strong link between feelings and facial expression. For example, if you smile long enough, eventually you'll feel happy instead of worried.

Relax specific body parts. Stage fright can affect various parts of the body. Here are some exercises to relax specific areas that might feel tense.

- *Relax your neck and throat.* Gently roll your neck from side to side, front to back, chin to chest, or all the way around.

- *Relax your shoulders.* Raise one or both shoulders as if you were shrugging. Then roll them back, then down, then forward. After a dozen or so repetitions, rotate in the opposite direction.

- *Relax your arms.* Shake out your arms, first only at the shoulders, then only at the elbow, finally letting your hands flop at the wrist.

- *Relax your hands.* Repeatedly clench and relax your fists. Start with an open hand and close each finger one by one to make a fist. Hold the position, then release.

Breathe deeply. Controlled breathing exercises are an effective way to lower your heart rate and calm down. The out-breath is the calming one; therefore, emphasize it and not the in-breath. Avoid breathing too fast or doing so much deep breathing that you hyperventilate. Try one or both of these techniques:

- *Emphatic out-breathing:* Breathe in through your nose. Then, breathe out through your mouth—with (1) an audible sigh; (2) a series of short bursts of air; or (3) one long, continuous stream of air.
- *Metered breathing:* Using a count of four, breathe in and out slowly and comfortably—four in and four out, like a metronome. Then, keeping the same measured pace, breathe in to the count of four, hold the breath to the count of four, and breathe out to the count of eight.

Prepare your voice. Some nervous symptoms affect your voice, causing you to feel short of breath or to produce a cracking or quivering sound. Here are some suggestions for keeping your voice in shape:

- *Practice diaphragmatic breathing.* Diaphragmatic breathing reduces strain on your vocal cords, slows your heart rate, and lowers your pitch. But where exactly is your diaphragm? To find it, put your hand on each of the following places: (1) belly (hand over the navel), (2) high chest (hand over the breastbone), and (3) diaphragm (hand on the bottom half of your rib cage). Now that you know where it is, think of your diaphragm as a balloon. Inhale slowly to make the balloon expand. Inflate it fully to reach your sides and back. Release your breath slowly and the balloon should deflate. Practice inflating and deflating the balloon for at least a minute, preferably lying on your back. (Page 149 has a link to a web demonstration.)
- *Rest and wake up your voice.* Try to get enough sleep the night before your talk. Wake up well before your presentation time to provide a natural warm-up period for your voice.
- *Use warmth to soothe your vocal cords.* (1) Take a long, hot shower, allowing the steam to revive a tired or irritated set of vocal cords. (2) Drink warm liquids, such as herbal tea or water with lemon, which will soothe your throat. Although warm liquids with caffeine are fine for your voice, they can increase your heart rate. Avoid warm milk or hot chocolate because dairy products tend to coat your vocal cords, which can cause problems when you present.
- *Do some vocal warm-ups.* Try humming. Begin slowly and quietly. Gradually add a full range of pitches. Then, practice making all the vowel sounds—"a, e, i, o, u."

3. Mental techniques

Some people find that mental relaxation techniques work better for them—that mental relaxation causes physical relaxation.

Try a positive approach. Decades ago, Dale Carnegie listed numerous ways to develop positive feelings about public speaking. One of the ideas, borrowed from psychologist William James, is to link feelings and actions. In other words, if you want to feel confident, then you should act confident. By doing so you can turn your adrenaline rush into positive energy, motivating the butterflies you feel in your stomach to fly in formation. To try this approach, act confident and repeat positive words or phrases before you present, such as "poised, positive, and prepared, poised, positive, and prepared."

Assess your style objectively. If you plan to record yourself, learn how to describe, rather than judge, your behaviors. Instead of saying "I looked pathetic in that fig leaf position," notice that your hands were clasped in front of you during the opening of your rehearsal. Then, change your thinking, either by refining your delivery behaviors or by accepting them as part of your style. To stay away from judgmental thinking, try one of the following approaches: (1) think rationally, as described next, or (2) create a positive self-image, as explained on the following page.

Think rationally. Psychologist Albert Ellis believed people could manage emotional reactions in a rational way. We've adapted his ABC approach so it applies to speech anxiety. The key is to reach "D," where you can dispute the emotional trap:

- A: Activating event (such as a nervous gesture or distracting movement) sparks an irrational . . .
- B: Belief system (such as "What a disaster" or "If I don't look perfect, then I'm terrible"), which causes . . .
- C: Consequences (such as speech anxiety or depression) that can be transcended by . . .
- D: Disputing the irrational belief system with rational thought (such as "Now that I'm aware of this gesture, I can work to gradually eliminate it" or "I don't demand perfection from other speakers so why do I demand it from myself?").

Create a positive self-image. Some speakers find that positive pictures work better than motivational words.

- *Visualize yourself as a successful speaker.* Act out the visualization in your head; see your upcoming talk, including your polished delivery behaviors and the favorable expressions on the faces in the audience. You may even want to hear their applause.
- *Look at a positive image.* Replay a recording of yourself giving a presentation. Stop at the point where you really like the image, where your delivery style looks natural and confident. Remember this image when it's time for your next presentation.
- *Imagine yourself as the guru.* To remind yourself that you know your subject matter, remember the times that you have impressed others with your knowledge. See yourself answering people's questions and fascinating them with new ideas.

Picture a calm scene. Relax by conjuring up an image of a pleasant scene. Learn how to take your mind from an everyday location to the relaxing place you have visualized.

- *Create a positive place.* On each of the several days before your presentation, close your eyes and imagine a beautiful, calm scene, such as the most beautiful beach you have ever visited. Add details to your image: see the various shades of blue, feel the temperature, and smell the air. Concentrate on your image, excluding everything else, and describe how you feel: "I feel warm and relaxed."
- *Juxtapose the stress.* Several days before your presentation, visualize the place where you are going to present. See the room and the audience; feel the stress. Then, distance yourself. Relax by visualizing the positive place you created for yourself.

Connect with the audience. Think of your audience as individuals and not a vast group of unknown faces. Remember that they are real people, who probably want you to succeed.

- *Meet them and greet them.* When people arrive, say "hello" and talk to a few of them. These brief greetings may help you relax.
- *"Befriend" the audience.* Even if you can't greet people in the room, try to think of them as individuals. Imagine having conversations with them. You may even want to think of them as potential friends, picturing them in your home, enthusiastically talking with them in a warm and pleasant atmosphere.

4. Last-minute tips

When it's actually time to deliver the presentation, try a few of the following relaxation techniques. Some of these suggestions can even be used as you speak.

Manage your physical symptoms. Obviously, you cannot start doing push-ups or practice humming when you are in the room waiting to present. Fortunately, there are a few subtle techniques you can use at the last minute to relax your body and help your voice:

- *Try isometric exercise.* These quick exercises can be used discretely to steady shaking hands or prevent tapping feet. Isometric exercises involve clenching and then quickly relaxing various muscles. For example, you might put your hands behind your back, tightly clench your fists, and then quickly relax your hands. Or, before you get up to speak, you might press or wiggle your feet against the floor, clench those muscles, and then relax your feet.

- *Take a deep breath.* Inhale slowly and deeply. Exhale completely. Imagine you are breathing in "the good" and out "the bad." A deep breath can slow your heart rate. Also use it to remind yourself that pausing gives you a chance to take in all the air your voice will need to make sound effectively.

- *Deal with a dry mouth.* If you suffer from a dry mouth, the most obvious solution is to sip water before you start to present and have a glass nearby as you present. When water isn't available, you can (1) gently nip the end of your tongue or (2) imagine sucking on a lemon slice—either one should cause your mouth to water.

Improve your mental state. Also, at the last minute, you can dispel stage fright by using what psychologists call "internal dialogue," which means, of course, talking to yourself. Here are some of the messages you may want to generate:

- *Give yourself a pep talk.* Act like a coach and deliver motivational messages to yourself, such as "I'm prepared and ready to do a great job. I can answer any question that comes my way." Or try a mantra such as "I can do this; I can do this."

- *Play up the audience's reception.* Look at the audience and find something positive to say about them, such as "These people are really going to be interested in what I have to say" or "They seem like a very friendly group."

Relax as you speak. Finally, here are four ways to relax while you are in front of your audience.

- *Speak to the interested listeners.* There are always a few kind souls in the audience who nod, smile, and react favorably. Especially early in the presentation, look at them and not at the people who are reading, staring out the window, or yawning. Seeing the engaged and friendly listeners will increase your confidence and soon you will feel able to look throughout the room.

- *Talk to someone in the back.* To make sure your voice sounds strong and confident, take a deep breath and talk to someone sitting in the back. Try to maintain this audible volume throughout your talk.

- *Know that you probably look and sound better than you feel.* Your nervousness is probably not as apparent to your audience as it is to you. Experiments show that even trained speech instructors do not see all the nervous symptoms speakers think they are exhibiting. Managers and students watching videotapes of their performances regularly say, "Hey, I look better than I thought I would!"

- *Concentrate on the here and now.* Focus on your ideas and your audience. Forget about past regrets and future uncertainties. You have already analyzed what to do—now just do it wholeheartedly.

In closing, we hope we have created an easy-to-follow guide that helps you prepare your presentation from start to finish. Whether you are an experienced presenter or just a beginner, we recommend that you:

- **AIM**, using the strategic framework described in Part I: analyze the audience, identify your intent, and make the most of the message.

- **Implement**, using the approach explained in Part II: craft the content, design the visuals, and refine your nonverbal delivery.

In addition to reading these chapters, use the index to find answers to your specific questions and refer to the bibliography to locate useful books, articles, and websites. And remember, you don't need to be perfect, but you do need to AIM.

BIBLIOGRAPHY

This bibliography serves both to acknowledge our sources and to provide readers with references for additional reading.

BOOKS AND ARTICLES

Aristotle, *The Art of Rhetoric*. New York: Penguin Books, 1991.

Atkinson, C., *Beyond Bullet Points,* 3rd ed., Redmond, WA: Microsoft Press, 2011.

_____*The Backchannel: How Audiences Are Using Twitter and Social Media and Changing Presentations Forever,* Berkeley, CA: New Rider, 2010.

Baney, J., *Guide to Interpersonal Communication.* Upper Saddle River, NJ: Prentice Hall, 2003.

Bolton, R., *People Skills: How to Assert Yourself, Listen to Others, and Resolve Conflicts.* New York: Simon & Schuster, 1989.

Buvala, K.S., *Measures of Story,* Tolleson, AZ: Creation Company Consultants, 2011.

Buzan, T. and B. Buzan, *The Mind Map Book.* London: Pearson Education, 2006.

Carnegie, D. *How to Develop Self-Confidence and Influence People by Public Speaking.* New York: Pocket Books, 1956.

Cialdini, R., *Influence: Science and Practice,* 5th ed. Boston: Allyn & Bacon, 2008.

Duarte, N., *slide:ology: The Art and Science of Creating Great Presentations.* Sebastopal, CA: O'Reilly Media, 2008.

___*Resonate: Present Visual Stories That Transform Audiences,* Hoboken, NJ: John Wiley & Sons, 2010.

Evans, P. and M. Thomas, *Exploring the Elements of Design*, 3rd ed. Clifton Park, NY: Thomson, 2012.

Few, S., *Show Me the Numbers: Designing Tables and Graphs to Enlighten.* Oakland, CA: Analytics Press, 2004.

___*Now You See It: Simple Visualization Techniques for Quantitative Analysis*, Oakland, CA: Analytics Press, 2009.

Flower, L., *Problem-Solving Strategies for Writing.* Fort Worth, TX: Harcourt Brace College Publishers, 2003.

French, J. and B. Raven, "The Bases of Social Power" in *Studies in Social Power,* D. Cartwright (ed.). Ann Arbor: University of Michigan Press, 1959.

Graham, L., *Basics of Design: Layout and Typography for Beginners*, 2nd ed. Clifton Park, NY: Thomson, 2006.

Heath, C. and D. Heath, *Made to Stick: Why Some Ideas Survive and Others Die.* New York: Random House, 2007.

_____*Switch: How to Change Things When Change Is Hard*, New York: Broadway Books, 2010.

Knapp, M. and J. Hall, *Nonverbal Communication in Human Interaction,* 7th ed. Belmont, CA: Thomson Wadsworth, 2010.

Kosslyn, S., *Graph Design for the Eye and Mind.* New York: Oxford University Press, 2006.

Linklater, K., *Freeing the Natural Voice: Image and Art in the Practice of Voice and Language,* 2nd ed. New York: Drama Publishers, 2006.

Medina, J., *Brain Rules: 12 Principles for Surviving and Thriving at Work, Home, and School.* Seattle, WA: Pear Press, 2008.

Minto, B., *The Minto Pyramid Principle: Logic in Writing and Thinking.* London: Minto International, Inc., 2007.

Munter, M., "Cross-Cultural Communication for Managers," *Business Horizons,* May/June, 1993.

—— *Guide to Managerial Communication: Effective Business Writing and Speaking,* 10th ed. Upper Saddle River, NJ: Prentice Hall, 2013.

—— and M. Netzley, *Guide to Meetings.* Upper Saddle River, NJ: Prentice Hall, 2002.

—— and D. Paradi, *Guide to PowerPoint.* Upper Saddle River, NJ: Prentice Hall, 2011.

Pink, D., *Drive: The Surprising Truth about What Motivates Us.* New York: Riverhead Books, 2009.

Rabinowitz, T., *Exploring Typography.* Clifton Park, NY: Thomson/Delmar Learning, 2006.

Reynolds, G., *Presentation Zen Design*, Berkeley, CA: New Riders, 2010.

Reynolds, S. and D. Valentine, *Guide to Cross-Cultural Communication,* 2nd ed. Upper Saddle River, NJ: Prentice Hall, 2010.

Roam, D., *Blah, Blah, Blah.* New York: Penguin Group, 2011.

Schenkler, I. and T. Herrling, *Guide to Media Relations.* Upper Saddle River, NJ: Prentice Hall, 2004.

Sedden, T. and J. Waterhouse, *Graphic Design for Non-Designers.* San Francisco: Chronicle Books, 2009.

Simmons, A., *Whoever Tells the Best Story Wins: How to Use Your Own Stories to Communicate with Power and Impact*, New York: AMACOM, 2007.

Sinek, S., *Start with Why: How Great Leaders Inspire Everyone to Take Action.* New York: Penguin Group, 2009.

Tannenbaum, R. and W. Schmidt, "How to Choose a Leadership Pattern," *Harvard Business Review,* March–April, 1958, 95–101.

Tufte, E., *The Cognitive Style of PowerPoint.* Cheshire, CT: Graphics Press, 2006.

White, J., *Color for Impact: How Color Can Get Your Message Across—or Get in the Way.* Berkeley, CA: Strathmoor Press, 1997.

Williams, R., *The Non-Designer's Design Book,* 3rd ed. Berkeley, CA: Peachpit Press, 2008.

Yates, J., "Persuasion: What the Research Tells Us," Cambridge, MA: Sloan School, Massachusetts Institute of Technology, 1992.

Zelazny, G., *Say It with Charts Complete Toolkit.* New York: McGraw-Hill, 2006.

—— *Say It with Presentations, How to Design and Deliver Successful Business Presentations,* 2nd ed. New York: McGraw-Hill, 2006.

INFORMATION ON THE WEB

Part 1: AIM Strategy

Page 7—*Assessment instruments:*

- For an overview of MBTI: http://www.myersbriggs.org/my-mbti-personality-type/mbti-basics/

- For an introduction to social styles: http://www.tracomcorp.com/training-products/model/social-style-model.html

Page 8—*Social media and the web:*

- To upload a video of your presentation: http://vimeo.com

- To upload your slides on the web: http://www.slideshare.net

Page 15—*Data-driven appeals:*

- For a humorous reminder that correlation is not causation, check out: http://www.businessweek.com/magazine/correlation-or-causation-12012011-gfx.html

- To test your skills in showing numbers clearly, go to Stephen Few's site: http://perceptualedge.com/files/GraphDesignIQ.html

Page 17—*Emotional appeals:*

- Watch statistician Hans Rosling humanize huge numbers and trends: http://www.gapminder.org/videos/hans-rosling-and-the-magic-washing-machine

- See emotional images linked to numbers: http://www.slideshare.net/mrcoryjim/smoke-the-convenient-truth-5602255
- Listen to author Susan Cain begin and end her talk about introverts with a personal story: http://www.thepowerofintroverts.com/about-the-book
- Hear economist Tyler Cowen's skeptical views about stories: http://www.ted.com/talks/tyler_cowen_be_suspicious_of_stories.html
- Find a link to an article by Chip and Dan Heath about "bright spots": http://www.heathbrothers.com/switch

Page 19—*Benefit statements:*

- Watch author Daniel Pink prove that benefits often need to be more than bonuses: http://www.ted.com/talks/dan_pink_on_motivation.html

Page 28—*The why focus of "sell" presentations:*

- Watch author Simon Sinek compare "why" to "how" and "what": http://www.ted.com/talks/simon_sinek_how_great_leaders_inspire_action.html

Page 32—*Knowledge-based targets:*

- To view a model that shows the many variations of understanding, go to Iowa State's center for learning and teaching: http://www.celt.iastate.edu/teaching/RevisedBlooms1.html

Page 39—*Multitasking myth* and *getting attention:*

- To learn more about hooking attention, look at Brain Rule #4 on John Medina's site (and rules 3, 5, 6, 9, and 10): http://brainrules.net/attention

Page 40—*Storytelling's complexity* and *Bill Gate's STAR moment:*

- To hear about the complexity of crafting stories, go to Sean Bulava's site: http://howtocreateastory.com/excerpts
- To view Bill Gate's star moment, go to: http://www.ted.com/talks/bill_gates_unplugged.html

Part 2: Implementation

Page 56—*Mind maps:*

- To see examples of mind maps, go to: http://www.thinkbuzan.com/us/support/mindmapgallery
- To download free mind mapping software, go to: http://freemind.sourceforge.net/wiki/index.php/Main_Page

Page 57—*Internet research:*

- For general searching tips, go to: www.lib.berkeley.edu/TeachingLib/ Guides/Internet/FindInfo.html
- For company searches, try: http://investing.businessweek.com/research/ company/overview/overview.asp and http://online.wsj.com/mdc/public/ page/marketsdata.html
- For economic data, try sites such as: data.gov, federalreserve.gov, and nber.org (National Bureau of Economic Research)
- For global data, try: www.worldbank.org and www.gapminder.org
- For a financial dictionary and articles, try: www.investopedia.com.

Page 60—*Visual thinking for storyboarding:*

- To learn how to visualize your ideas, go to Dan Roam's site: danroam.com
- To watch a demonstration of his visual imagination: http://vimeo. com/38273833

Page 80—*Image-driven slides:*

- To see samples of Garr Reynold's image-driven slides, go to: http:// www.slideshare.net/garr/sample-slides-by-garr-reynolds
- For slide design tips, explore his website: presentationzen.com

Page 101—*Charts:*

- Stephen Few's website is full of useful articles about charts. To see before and after examples: http://www.perceptualedge.com/examples.php
- Also look at his chart selection matrix: http://www.perceptualedge.com/ articles/misc/Graph_Selection_Matrix.pdf

Pages 106–108—*Photos, maps,* and *animation:*

- To find free photos, visit: morguefile.com.
- To learn about creative commons and how you can legally use and cite Flickr photos, watch Alvin Trusty's video: http://vimeo.com13248511
- To learn about public domain, go to: www.publicdomainsherpa.com
- To use free maps: http://www.openstreetmap.org
- To see how designer Nancy Duarte uses animation and transitions to accentuate her message, go to: http://blog.duarte.com/2010/01/5-ways-to-make-powerpoint-sing-and-dance

Page 110—*Overcoming wordiness and using active voice:*

- For financial examples, use the SEC's Plain Language Handbook: http://www.sec.gov/pdf/handbook.pdf

- For more examples, go to the government's plain language website, where you can download a different guide and find tools such as this list of how to simplify words: http://www.plainlanguage.gov/howto/word-suggestions/simplewords.cfm

Page 116—*Eliminating chartjunk:*

- To see how designer Jan Schultink fixes a PowerPoint column chart, go to: http://blog.ideatransplant.com/2012/04/fixing-standard-data-charts.html

Page 117—*Citing sources:*

- For deck citations: http://library.hbs.edu/guides/citationguide/pdf

- To attribute creative commons images: http://vimeo.com13248511

Pages 138 to 140—*Power poses, diaphragmatic breathing, and rational thinking:*

- Watch Professor Amy Cuddy explain how and why to use expansive non-verbal behaviors: http://poptech.org/popcasts/amy_cuddy_power_poses

- Locate your diaphragm and see a demonstration of proper breathing: http://cmhc.utexas.edu/stressrecess/animations/diaphramatic_breathing/diaphragmatic_breathing.html

- Read more about Albert Ellis and his rational ABC approach at: http://rebtnetwork.org

Index

A

Action-based targets, 31–32
Active listening, 71
Active voice, 110, 149
Accent color, 89. *See also* Spot color
Agenda: *See* Preview
Agenda slide, 81; using animation for, 108; using as section visual, 113
AIM Strategy: framework for, 2; defined, 3, as mnemonic, 47
Alignment: for message titles, 95; for photograph placement, 107; for text boxes as chart labels, 116
Animation (to build information on slides), 108, 132, 148
Appeals (for persuasion), 15–17. *See also* Benefit statements and Credibility
Area charts, 100
Aristotle, 20, 144
Arm gestures, 122
Arrows, 103, 105, 114
Asking for less: as persuasive technique, 17
Asking for more: as persuasive technique, 17
Atkinson, Cliff, 46, 77, 80, 144
Attainable targets, choosing, 33
Attitude (of speaker): toward questions and answers, 69; toward speech anxiety, 140–141
Attractiveness (credibility), 22
Audience: analysis of primary, 5–7; analysis of secondary, 8; attention, hook the, 38–40; expectations and knowledge of, 9–12; feelings and bias of, 13–14; opinion about culture, 12; persuasion of, 15–23; reactions to color choice, 12, 87–88; RESIST distractions of, 40; speaker's credibility with, 10, 20–21; techniques for difficult, 75; techniques for hostile, 75–76; ways gesturing affects, 123; ways dress affects, 129; ways to interact with, before speaking, 132–134, 141, 143
Audience filter (for creating benefit statements), 18, 19
Authority, to build credibility, 20
Autocorrect options (turning off in PowerPoint), 111, 112

B

Backchannel: advantages/ disadvantages, 76; dealing with, 76–77; *See also* Online comments
Backchannel, the, 77, 144
Background: colors for, 88; design for, 96
Backward look/forward look transitions, 66, 68
Bandwagon appeal, 16
Baney, Joann, 128, 144
Bar charts, 101,102, 103; ways to eliminate chartjunk on, 115, 116
Benchmarking, 16, 19, 22
Benefit statements (for audience): 18–19, 147; targeted to decision makers, 23; solution based scenario for; 58

Best practices, 16
Beyond Bullet Points, 80, 144
Bias (of audience), 14
Black slides: as background choice,
    88, 96; as closing visual, 82;
    to connect with audience, 83;
    for photograph background,
    107; as way to eliminate old
    news, 132; as way to end slide
    show, 133
Blah, Blah, Blah, 105, 145
"Blanding it out": (on message
    titles), 86
Body language, 120–125, 135. *See
    also* Nonverbal delivery
Bolton, Robert, 70, 144
Bottom line: as part of direct
    approach, 41
Brain Rules, 38, 145, 147
Breaks: during presentations, 47;
    for online interactions, 77;
    from overuse of visuals, 83;
    pausing for, 47; Q&A
    interactions for, 47; schedule
    for, 47; of text lines on
    visuals, 112
Breathing: improving, 139, 149;
    tips for last minute, 142
Bridging technique, 72
"Bright spots" (persuasion
    technique), 17, 147
Bubble charts, 101,102; using
    animation to display, 108
"Build" technique, 108, 132, 148
Bullet characters, 95
Bullet lists; arranging Slide Master
    for, 95; building, 108; limiting
    109, maintaining parallelism
    with 110–111, ways to make
    more visual, 112
Buvala, Sean, 39, 144, 147
Buzon, Tony, 56, 144

C
Capital letters (avoiding overuse
    of), 95, 112; turning off
    autocorrect feature for, 112;
    See also Case
Cartoons, 108
Carnegie, Dale, 140, 144
Case (choice of), 111
Centering titles, 95
Channel (of communication):
    cultural aspects of, 12; as
    medium for message 37;
Character (credibility): 10, 22
Charts (for data and numbers):
    audience's need for accurate
    design of, 15, 146; design of,
    100–102, 148; determining
    color for parts of, 114;
    eliminating chartjunk on,
    115, 116; *See also* Visual
    aids
Chartjunk (avoiding), 115–116,
    149
Chevron diagrams, 103, 104, 105
Chunking information, 43–45;
    audience attention and, 45; as
    way to think about visuals, 82
Cialdini, Robert, 16, 21, 144
Closing (for presentation), 67–68;
    making visuals for, 82; what
    not to say, 2, 67
Color: audience expectations
    about, 12, 87; background for
    visuals, 88; choosing scheme
    for, 87–91; contrasting
    text and background, 89;
    dimming, 89; editing use of
    114, 115, 116; logo, 96, 98;
    in photographs, 106; Power-
    Point custom, 90–91; spot, 89,
    91, 114 testing, in room, 133;
    testing on large screen, 91, 133

Column charts, 100, 101; adding
    emphasis on 114; eliminating
    chartjunk on, 116
Common ground, 21
Communicating in interactive
    situations, 29. *See also*
    Question and answer
Company templates, 98
Competence (credibility), 10,
    21–22
Complimentary colors, 91
Component comparison (charts),
    101, 102
Conceptual parallelism, 110–111
Consistency reminders (persuasive
    technique), 16, 17, 19
Consult/join situations, defined,
    26; general purpose of, 29;
Contrast-based structure, 43, 44;
    for tell presentation, 64
Copyright (photographs), 106
Correlation comparison (charts),
    101, 102, 146
Creative commons, 106, 148, 149
Credibility: analyzing, 10; cultural
    affects on, 12; as persuasion
    technique, 15, 20–21
Cropping (photographs) 106–107
Cuddy, Amy, 138, 149
Culture: audience expectations
    based on, 12; effect of, on
    color choice, 12, 87; effect
    of, on dress, 129; effect of,
    on use of gestures, 12, 123;
    effect of, on direct approach,
    12; effect of, on using
    indirect approach, 42; effect
    of, on question and answer
    sessions, 11, 69; effect of,
    on time, 12; effect of, on
    visuals, 12; strategy for, 12
Circular flows diagram, 103–105
Cuddy, Amy, 138, 149
Custom color screen, 90, 91, 99
Cycle (diagram), 104, 105

D
Data-driven appeals, 15, 146
Data dump, of ideas, 56, 61
Decks, 79; background color
    for, 88–89; challenges of,
    134; compared to slides,
    80; designing Slide Master
    for, 98; font sizes for,
    94; including message
    titles in, 81–86; including
    page numbers in, 97, 117;
    including sources in, 117;
    presenting techniques with,
    133–134; testing colors for,
    91; as written material to
    another presentation, 50
Delivery: practice techniques to
    improve, 130–135; relaxation
    techniques for, 136–143
Delivery (nonverbal): body
    language for, 120–125; of
    closing message, 67; cultural
    influences on, 12; use of
    space and objects for, 129;
    vocal traits for, 125–128
Design Themes, 99; *See also*
    Templates
Diaphragmatic breathing, 139,
    149
Difficult audience members,
    75–76
Dimming options, 89
Direct approach, 41–42; in
    opening, 63
Distorted paraphrases, 74
"Distracters" (difficult audience
    members), 75
"Don't know" (questions), 74
"Door-in-the-face," (persuasion
    technique), 17
Dot charts, 101, 102
Dress, 11, 129
Dry mouth, 2, 136, 137, 142
Duarte, Nancy, 39, 80, 96, 144,
    148

E

Elevator pitch, 59
Ellis, Albert, 140, 149
Email: to gather audience information, 5; as technique for focusing, 59
Emotional appeals (persuasion technique), 17, 146, 147
Emotions (of audience), 13; as attention-getting technique, 39-40; as part of objective, 31–33
Emphasis: of key ideas, 39, 41, 47; pausing for, 125; using color for, 114
Empty chair (question), 74
Enunciation, 127
Equipment: choosing font size based on, 94; practicing with, 133, 135
Executive summary (in decks), 82
Exercises (for relaxation), 138–139
Expertise: dealing with mixed levels of, 9; enhancing credibility by referring to, 20
Eye contact: for listening, 70; for presenting, 124; when using visual aids, 132

F

Facial expression, 125
False premise (question), 74
Family (fonts), 93
Features vs. benefits, 18–19
Feedback, requesting presentation, 137
Few, Stephen, 144, 146
Filler words (avoiding), 128
Flagging technique, 39, 72
Flower, Linda, 59, 144
Focusing techniques, 59, 82. See also Objective
Font (choosing), 92–94; comparison of size in slides/decks, 99

"Foot-in-the-door" (persuasion technique), 17
Formality: audience expectations about, 11; effect of, on space and objects, 128; effect of, on stance, 121; effect of, on visual aids, 80
Format, audience expectations about, 11
French, John 21, 144
Fruit salad effect (avoiding), 91, 99

G

Gatekeepers, 22; creating benefit statements for, 23
Gates, Bill, 38, 57, 147
Gantt diagrams, 103, 104
Gestures: analyzing, 122–123; relaxation for, 139
Goodwill credibility, 21
Google (research tips), 57
Grabber (in presentation opening), 38, 63
Graham, Lisa, 95, 145
Grayscale: for logos, 96; for photographs, 107
Grid (in PowerPoint), 97
Guide to PowerPoint, 90, 145

H

Halo effect (credibility), 22
Hand gestures: analyzing, 122–123; relaxation for, 138
Handouts: as added medium, 50; background color for, 88; font sizes for, 94
Headings (on visual aids), 81–86
Heath, Dan and Chip, 17, 145, 147
Height, 129
Highlighting: on visuals, 114
Hostile questioning, 75–76
Honeycomb diagrams, 103, 104
Hooking attention, 38–40
Humor, 10, 63
Hypothetical (question), 74

I
Idea charts, 60, 61, 103
Image-driven slides, 80, 109, 147, 148
Importance-based structure, 44; for sell presentation, 65
Indirect approach, 42; in opening, 62
Inflection (vocal), 127
Intent (as cultural differences), 12
Intent (of presentation), 25–35
Interactive situation, communicating in, 29
Interest (of audience), 13
Internet: researching with, 57, 148
Isometric exercises, 142
Item comparison (charts), 101, 102

J
Jargon, 9, 21
Join situations: vs. consult situations, 26; defined, 25; general purpose of, 29

K
Knowledge-based targets, 31, 32, 147

L
Labels, on charts, 115, 116; colors for, 89; font size for, 94; use of text box to create 105, 116
Layering (communication efforts), 51
Left-justified titles, 95
Legends (on charts), avoiding, 116
Legibility (fonts), 92
Lettering: colors for, 89; legibility of, 92; sizing for, 94, 99
Letterjunk (avoiding), 95
Line charts, 100, 101; eliminating chartjunk in, 115, 116
Line spacing, 95, 99

Lingo, 9, 21
Listening skills, 70–71
Loaded language (question), 74
Logos, 88, 96, 98

M
Maps, 108, 148
Margins, 97; on decks, 98
Master view (in PowerPoint), 87; *See also* Slide Master
Matrix diagrams, 103, 104
Medina, John, 38, 46, 145, 147
Medium of communication: defined, 37, selecting the most effective, 48–51
Meeting (instead of presentation), 29, 48
Memory, 38, 46–47; creating information chunks, 43–44
Mental relaxation techniques, 140–141, 142
Message strategy, 37–51
Message titles: composing, 84–85; influencing design decisions, 86; influence on font choice, 94; linking to, with spot color and highlighting, 114; value of, on visuals, 46
Microblogs, 76
Mind maps, 34, 56, 57, 147
Minimal encouragers, 70
Minto, Barbara, 60, 145
Mnemonic devices, 47
Munter, Mary, 145
Myers-Briggs Type Indicator (MBTI), 7, 146

N
Needlers, (difficult audience members), 75
Nervousness (dealing with), 136–143
Nitpickers, (difficult audience members), 75

Nonverbal (listening skills), 70
Nonverbal (delivery skills): body
    language for, 120–125;
    managing nervous symptoms
    of, 136–142; messages,
    considering, 134; use of
    space and objects for, 129;
    vocal traits for, 125–128
Notepages in slide presentation,
    130
Notes (speaking from), 130
Nutshell technique, 59, 82

O

Objective (for presentation):
    creating, 30–33; drafting,
    59; examples of, 33; sticking
    with, during Q&A, 35, 72;
    as tool for creating visuals,
    82; tying to, in closing, 35,
    68; using, to stay focused,
    34–35, 59
Online comments, 76–77
Online: presentation, preparation
    for, 135
Open-ended questions, 70
Opening: stance for, 121; wording
    for, 62–63
Opinion: assess people's, about
    target, 32
Opinion leaders, 22; creating
    benefit statements for, 23
Organization (for presentation),
    64–66
Organizational charts, 105
Outline: to order content, 60;
    using, as notes, 130

P

Page numbers, 97, 117, 134,
    135
Parallelism, 110–111
Paragraph spacing, 95, 99

Paraphrasing (during Q&A),
    71–73, when distorted, 74;
    when handling hostility, 76
Pauses, 47, 67, 126, 128
Persuasion: techniques for, 15–23
Photographs, 106–107, 112, 148
Physical relaxation techniques,
    138–139
Picture superiority effect, 46
Pie charts, 101, 102; avoiding
    chartjunk in, 115, 116
Pitch. *See* Inflection
Pitchbooks, 79; *See also* Decks
Placeholders (in PowerPoint),
    97, 98
Point size, 93, 94, 99
"Pointer" (using PowerPoint as),
    114
Pontificators (difficult audience
    member), 75
Positive thinking, 140–142
Posture: for listening, 70; for
    presentations, 120–121
Power pose for relaxation, 138,
    149
PowerPoint: adding animation
    with, 108, 148; as common
    tool, 79; creating notepages
    in, 130; creating records
    with, 85; custom color screen
    in, 90; designing decks with,
    98; designing a Slide Master
    in, 87–99; designing Title
    Master in, 98; eliminating
    chartjunk defaults in, 116;
    ending slide shows with,
    133; inserting photographs
    with, 107; making diagrams
    with, 103, 105; making line
    charts with, 100; making
    text charts with, 109–112;
    modifying placeholders in,
    97; starting with titles in,
    84–86; template traps in, 99

Practice: to avoid nervousness, 136–137; with slides, 132–133; techniques for, 130–135;

Presentation objective: defined 30; examples of, 33; how to use, 34–35; how to write 30–32. *See also*, Objective

Presentations: audience analysis for, 5–23; intent and objectives for, 24–35; introduction to scope of, 62; message and medium for, 36–51; nonverbal delivery skills for, 118–135; pros and cons of, 49; Q&A during, 69–77; relaxation techniques for, 136–142; requesting feedbacks for, 137; strategy for, 3; craft content for, 54–68; visual aids for, 79–117

Presentation Zen Design, 80, 145

Presenter View in slide presentation, 130, 133

Preview (oral): chunking to create, 45; in a deck presentation, 133; as part of opening, 63

Preview (visual): definition of, 63; to reinforce your structure, 81; use of, between sections in slide shows, 113

Primary audience, 6–7

Private conversations (instead of presentation), 48

Problem/solution (as sell structure), 65

Public domain, 106, 148

Purpose (of presentation), 25–35

Pyramid diagrams, 103, 104; using animation to build, 108

Q

Question and answers: audience expectations about 11, 69;

closing after, 68; creating visuals for, 83; preparing for, 69–77

R

Rate (vocal), 126–127

Raven, Bertram, 21, 144

Readability (of fonts), 95; based on font style 92, 93, 95; based on point size, 94, 99; linked to color, 89; of text lines on deck pages, 98

Recall, improving, 46–47

Reciprocal concessions (as persuasion technique), 17

Rehearsal: general techniques for, 130–135; to overcome nervousness, 131; with slides, 132–133

Relaxation (techniques for), 136–142

Retention, structure for, 46

Reynolds, Garr, 80, 145, 148

Research techniques, 57

RGB values, 90

Roam, Dan, 60, 145, 148

Room, practicing in, 131, 133

Rosling, Hans, 17, 146

Rulers (in PowerPoint), 97

S

Sans serif fonts, 92, 93

Say It With Charts, 100, 105, 145

Scheduling a meeting (instead of presentation), 48

Screenwriting approach (for opening), 62

Seating arrangement: choices for, 129; positions for, 121, 134

Secondary audience, 6, 8

Section visuals, 81; as break from visuals, 83; background layout for, 88

Sell presentations: audience's
involvement in; 28; closings
for, 67–68; defined, 26–28;
examples of, 66; general
purpose of, 28; organizing,
65; problems/solutions
structure for, 65; purposes
and objectives for, 33;
question and answer sessions
for, 28; why focus of, 28, 147
Serif vs. sans serif fonts, 92
Similarity (as part of credibility), 22
Simmons, Annette, 58, 145
Slideshare.net, 8, 146
Slide Layouts, 97
Slides: background for, 88, 96;
color choices for text, 89;
compared to decks, 80;
designing template for,
87–97; font size for, 94;
making message titles for,
84–86; rehearsal with, 132–
133; testing, 91, 117. *See
also* PowerPoint
slide:ology, 80, 144
Slide Master (in PowerPoint), 87–99
SmartArt, 105
Smiling, 125, 138
Social media, 8, 76–77, 146
Solution-based scenario: for
benefit statements, 58;
example of, 58
Space: as basis for structuring, 44,
65; cultural affect on, 12; in
presentations, 129
Spot color, 87, 89, 91, 114
Stakeholders, 8
Stalling techniques, 74
Stance (for speaking), 120–121
Stand-alone sense (in visual aids),
85, 110
STAR moment, 39, 47
Sticky notes, 60; shown as
ordering technique, 61

Storyboards: example of, 61;
method for using, 60; as
starting place for visuals, 82;
visual thinking of, 60
Storytelling, 17, 39, 58, 147
Structural patterns, selecting, 44,
64–65
Structure: choosing direct vs.
indirect, 41–42; creating
information chunks for, 43;
deciding what to say for,
62–68; flow of, explaining,
45; focusing for, 59; ordering
for, 60; using visuals to
reinforce, 81–83, 113

T
Table of contents, 81; delivering
preview based on, 133;
editing, 117
T charts, 103, 104
Targets (for presentation
objective), 31–32
Tell situations: audience's
involvement in; 27; defined,
26–28; closings for, 67–68;
general purpose of, 27;
organizing, 64; purposes
and objectives for, 33;
question and answer sessions
for, 27
Templates (for PowerPoint),
avoiding prepared, 87;
making 87–89; working with
company-provided, 98
Text box, 105, 116
3D (avoiding on charts), 115, 116
Time-based structure, for tell
presentations, 44, 64
Time lines (diagrams) 103, 104
Time series comparison, 100, 101
Timing: audience expectations
about, 11; cultural attitude
toward, 12; factoring into

objective, 34; practicing for, 130–131
Titles (on visual aids): composing, 81–86; font size for, 94
Title case, 111
Title Master, 98
Title slide, 81; *See also* Title Master
Topic titles (avoiding), 84–85
Topical structure, 44; for sell presentations, 65; for tell presentations, 64
Trackers (to reinforce structure), 113, 117
TRACOM social styles, 7, 146
Transitions: backward look/ forward look, 66, 68; explicit use of, 66; practicing out loud, 131; using section visuals for, 81, 83; using on slides, 108
Tufte, Edward, 115, 146
Typeography, 92– 95

V
Venn diagram, 103, 104, 105
Visual aids: audience expectations about, 11, 12; chart design for, 100–102; diagram design for, 103–105; editing, 113–117; highlighting in 114;

message titles on, 46, 81–86; photographs for, 106–107; for presentation preview, 63, 81; reinforcing, 47; template design for, 86–99
Visuals: *See* Visual Aids
Visualization (to relax), 141
Voice: analyzing traits for, 125–128; relaxing, 139
Volume, 125–126

W
Welcome slide in online presentation, 135
Western business culture, 12
White, Jan, 91, 146
WIIFM ("what's in it for me"), 18–19
Word Art (avoiding), 112
Wordiness (avoiding), 109–110
Writing (instead of presentation), 48–49

X
X-height, 93, 94, 95, 99

Y
Yates, JoAnne, 16, 111, 146

Z
Zelazny, Gene, 100, 105, 145